From Bondage
To Liberty

Dance, Children, Dance

From Bondage To Liberty

Dance, Children, Dance

Jim Rayburn III

MORNINGSTAR PRESS
Colorado Springs, Colorado

First printing 2000

ISBN 0-9673897-4-7

LCCN 99-75252

Material taken from *He That is Spiritual*, copyright 1918 by Lewis Sperry Chafer, copyright 1967 by Zondervan Publishing House, is used by permission.

Quotations taken from *He That Is Spiritual* by Lewis Sperry Chafer, copyright 1918 by Lewis Sperry Chafer, copyright 1967 by Zondervan Publishing House, are used by permission.

Material taken from *Young Life's Malibu*, copyright 1984 by Elsie G. Campbell, is used by permission.

First printing, titled *Dance, Children, Dance*, Tyndale House Publishers, October, 1984

ATTENTION CORPORATIONS, UNIVERSITIES, COLLEGES, AND PROFESSIONAL ORGANIZATIONS: Quantity discounts are available on bulk purchases of this book for educational purposes. Special books or book excerpts can also be created to fit specific needs. For information, please contact Morningstar Press, 1947 Forest Ridge Drive, Colorado Springs, CO 80918, ph. 719-548-9592.

TO JIM,
WHOSE COMPASSION, WARMTH,
HUMOR, WIT, RUGGED INDIVIDUALISM,
AND RAGING LOVE AFFAIR WITH DEITY
ARE ALL TOO SELDOM SEEN.

ALSO TO MAXINE,
FOR HER HONESTY, SENSITIVITY, AND
WILLINGNESS TO EXPOSE THE DEPTH
OF HER OWN STRUGGLES THAT OTHERS
MIGHT BENEFIT.

LASTLY, TO THE MANY WONDERFUL
PEOPLE WHO HAVE MADE THE YOUNG LIFE
WORK POSSIBLE, ACROSS THE U.S.A.
AND AROUND THE WORLD, PAST
AND PRESENT, WHO HAVE CARRIED
ON AND CONTINUE TO CARRY ON
THE VITALLY IMPORTANT WORK
THAT WAS BIRTHED THROUGH JIM
AND MAXINE RAYBURN. YOUR
NAMES WOULD NUMBER
IN THE THOUSANDS. MAY GOD
RICHLY BLESS YOU ALL.

ACKNOWLEDGMENTS

MY special thanks to Lucia, Shannon, and Michelle, who gave so much and asked for so little, and without whose love, faith, and support this project would not have been possible.

To Wally Urban, Dick Halverson, Bill and Bea Mitchell, William and Marge Andrews, Donna Johnson, Kyle du Ford, Elsie Lane, Tyndale House Publishers, and "About Books," a most heartfelt thank-you. Some of you have gone on to be with the Lord you loved, but your various contributions to this project will not be forgotten.

TABLE OF CONTENTS

JIM RAYBURN was one of the few authentic heroes in my life. From our first meeting to the last, he was for me the prototype of what a servant of Christ should be. He relished life. His gutsy courage was legendary. His ability to communicate the love of God in Christ was simply incomparable. His spontaneous humor, which seemed always to lie very near the surface, was never irrelevant or out of place. Its sheer naturalness was always integral to his speech, the antithesis of the sort of artificial humor that is dragged in to get a laugh or is used for the sake of comedy relief.

More often than not, Jim made his point in ways that evoked sheer delight and profound insight simultaneously. He was the master iconoclast who was totally unimpressed with pretension and pomposity. He was the incarnation of God's love in Christ, and he communicated that love in attitude and action as well as in word. His devotion to Christ was contagious.

Biographers sometimes go to one extreme or the other especially when the subject is a next of kin. The subject is portrayed as a saint, whose life was above criticism, virtually infallible, one with whom the reader is unable to identify. Or the subject is portrayed as a character without virtue, one in whom the reader would find little, if anything, to emulate.

Jim Rayburn III has avoided both extremes. He simply records facts about a father and mother who struggled, often with questionable success, to nurture their marriage and family. It is the story of a devoted couple who suffered almost beyond belief and human endurance. Despite this, they remained true to Christ and to one another.

Here is the record of a pilgrimage with Christ which will inspire, instruct, awe, amaze, and motivate its readers. Congratulations as you embark on this unforgettable adventure.

Richard C. Halverson
Chaplain, United States Senate
July 18, 1984

I HAVE often heard it said that every family has a skeleton or two in the closet. If in the public eye, one family might decide to expose those skeletons while another would defend its public image, and honor, at any cost. This was an issue I had to face in writing this story. It was a tough issue, frankly, for no family likes to expose its dirty laundry in public. Yet, I knew that no one could ever tell the true story of Jim and Maxine Rayburn without revealing some things we're not proud of. Someone else might tell bits and pieces of this story, but no one could give the inside account revealed here.

A friend encouraged me to "clean this up" and make it more of a promotional piece for the work my father left behind. But this account wasn't written to be a promotional piece, or to please any person, persons, or groups. It was written to record the facts about the lives of Jim and Maxine Rayburn, warts and all. I knew that an "up close and personal" exposure to Jim would serve as an inspiration to readers beyond anything I might be encouraged to fabricate, or modify.

This is a story that might shock some readers. If you have normal human emotions it will likely make you cry, as well as laugh. In places, it is not a pretty story. But it is a truthful narrative about a most remarkable, unusual man, and the woman he married. I am their son, and the events I've recorded here were happenings to which I was an eyewitness (save for those that took place before I was on the scene).

In writing the first edition of this book, published by Tyndale House Publishers, as well as this revised version published sixteen years later, I gained a tremendous awareness that in telling this narrative, I was standing on Holy Ground. From day one this project was inspired by God, blessed by God, and anointed by God. It was a true privilege to be used by Him and inspired by Him to author this historical account. Hopefully, that's how it was; God was the author and I was the instrument. That is truly how it seemed, and that's the only way I ever wanted it.

Jim Rayburn's legacy goes on, of course, in his children, grand-children, and great-grandchildren, through his diaries, writings, and tapes, through the work of Young Life and many other outfits that are staffed by people Jim influenced, through many churches that have hired pastors trained in Young Life, and through the Jim Rayburn Foundation. It would truly be impossible to measure the impact that Jim had upon this world; his disciples are scattered over every continent on the globe (with the possible exception of Antarctica).

It is my sincere hope that you find this account not only an interesting read, but an inspiration as well. May it be a stepping stone to a deeper, richer, freer, more exciting, and more intimate relationship with God. Both Jim and Maxine would have wanted it that way.

For further information or materials, contact me at the address below:

Jim Rayburn (III)
www.jimrayburn.com
e-mail: jimrayburn@compuserve.com

Roots - Starched and Ironed

IMITATING his traveling evangelist father, young Jim, age two and a half, looked down from the tabletop on which he was standing, shook his finger in the air, and struggled for the words, "All be good. All be good!" The guests who had gathered for this performance laughed and nodded their approval. Young "Jamie" seemed destined to make a fine preacher-man, his parent's choice of all possible professions.

Jamie was born in Marshalltown, Iowa, July 21, 1909, but shortly afterward his parents packed up and headed for Newton, Kansas. Newton was the railroad crossroads to all points North, South, East, and West, and the ideal spot to come and go for a man who made his living on the road.

Young Jim's (Jamie's) childhood years were rich in the adventures of youth as he and his three younger brothers, Paul, Robert, and Frank, together challenged their folk's ability to properly raise four such fun-seeking, mischievous, and charismatic boys. Summers were spent at the vacation home in Buena Vista, Colorado.

Outside of school, Jim's early life was centered around the First Presbyterian Church in Newton. Life was an endless routine of Sunday school meetings, church camps, youth group gatherings, Bible studies, choir practices, and prayer meetings. In short, Jim's family went to church whenever the doors were open.

1

Sunday was a holy day in Jim's household; one was not permitted to read, work, or play until Monday arrived. The only book one could read on Sunday was the Bible. Since work was not allowed, meals for the holy day were prepared on Saturday. Playing any kind of game, and there were very few that weren't considered sinful, was strictly forbidden. Jim was finally allowed to play catch with a baseball (after much family discussion), but there was to be no hitting, no running, and no shouting. Using the bat to hit the ball was absolutely forbidden, a breach of God's ways. Having fun on holy day required punishment, which served to appease an angry god. Come Monday, however, God himself became a baseball fan. One could play all the baseball he had time for, and with God's blessing to boot.

To Jim the whole concept of divine goodness was lost in the drudgery of religion. God seemed to be a narrow-minded antagonist, rather than a spiritual being whose very essence is love. Nevertheless, it was called the "Christian life," and Jim was expected to follow it.

Jim's mother could have doubled for Carrie Nation (one of her heroines) or perhaps a United States Marine Corps recruiter. What she lacked in physical stature was made up for in rigid personality. Not known for possessing tolerance or patience, she viewed any kind of weakness as sin.

Mother Rayburn was very competitive, and instilled in her children this same fire. She would rise extra early Tuesday mornings to be the first woman on the block with her laundry hanging on the clothesline. It seemed important to her that the other housewives made note of her victory. She taught them the "Christian" way on laundry day. It was based on the belief that God loves a hard worker far more than one who sleeps an extra hour.

Jim's parents had themselves been products of very strict, religious upbringings. His mother had come from a home where those who knocked on the door were greeted with a verse of Scripture. For her, childhood had contained little love, and absolutely no freedom. Words of love were simply mixed with dutiful obligations, and then presented to the children under the label of Christianity.

By constitution and conviction, Jim was unable to reproduce the kind of joyless Christianity his parents enforced. But like many other children so instructed, Jim grew up with a ton of guilt in his backpack. It was a heavy load to carry, and for most of his life he struggled with the weight of it, for it's difficult to dance with too much weight in one's pack.

Young Jim was not to be known as a preacher-man; in both his appearance and his approach to discipleship he had no regard for the traditional role. Nor did he arrive at "being good," at least not in the external sense of his mother's understanding. But his was a life that influenced thousands, and deeply affected my own. There are those who feel Jim was a prophet, and others say a saint. Some have called him a sinner, dreamer, and a revolutionary. I called him Dad.

A quest for high adventure followed Jim throughout his life, and seasoned every aspect of it. It seems he split, cracked, or shattered every other bone in his body in pursuit of excitement, be it challenging the white water rapids, exploring an abandoned mine, hanging by rope to the side of a cliff, snow skiing or water skiing, ditching a policeman in a highway chase, or jumping off a windswept cornice to a vertical snow field far below. When asked if he had any regard for his safety, Jim always replied, "My activities are just as safe as sitting in church, probably safer."

That such a man would make his mark upon the world with a spiritual legacy seems too good to be true, for he resembled a man of the cloth as Madonna does a Catholic nun. But much of Jim's adult life was to be lived in conflict. The battle to separate the insights in his heart from the ways of his folks would be a long and difficult ordeal. To follow his heart and ignore the rules was to jeopardize his standing with God. To accept the ways of his parents, however, was to make a mockery of God within his own heart. "The problem with me," Jim would later express, "is that I got starched and ironed before I got washed."

It is said that truth is stranger than fiction. The story of Jim's life will support that. He was a man who had a love affair with Jesus Christ, a man who pioneered a revolutionary movement within an often stagnant religious system, and a man whose warmth and love

3

inspired thousands. Yet, he would die a lonely, ridiculed, and rejected man, scorned by many of the people he most loved.

His story begins with Helen Maxine Stanley, a pretty, enigmatic young woman with a soft heart and a free spirit.

Romance

UNLIKE Jim's family, whose entire life was a progression of evange-listic meetings, Maxine's folks showed little personal interest in things spiritual or religious. They did ask their young daughter to attend the closest Sunday school, but outside of that responsibility she grew up with much freedom to do as she pleased. Even as a young child, she was allowed to leave the house and spend the day alone in the streets of Kansas City. As her parents struggled with a dying mar-riage, she was largely ignored. Max found that a dime paid to the local movie house allowed her an all day stay.

When Max was fourteen, her life was changed forever. Return-ing from school, she found a note from her mother on the piano bench:

Dear Max,
I've gone away. Don't try to find me.
Mom

How is one to understand such a note from a mother? There was no expression of love nor any attempt to explain.

Max was soon sent to the home of her mother's sister. While lying in bed at night, she could overhear the conversations in the living room. Much of what she heard was painful— "What shall we do with Maxine? We can't shoot her." Confused, bewildered, feeling unwanted, Max never again felt secure, safe, and appreciated. Her self-image was shattered; she had lost her innocence!

Shuffled from home to home, Max was not to find acceptance. Abandoned by her mother, unwanted by others, she felt the deep, searing pain of a broken heart. To escape her pain, Max made up fantasies in which she was wanted and appreciated. No fantasy was sweeter than that of meeting the prince who would take her away from her miserable existence, to a place where he would love and cherish her forever.

It was a strange twist of destiny that led Jim's path across Maxine's. She was a street urchin from the city; he was a small-town church-boy. His family was stable but restrictive. Her family, though once fun loving, was now broken and dispersed. Jim was happy, positive, and assertive; Max was unhappy, skeptical, and timid. In almost every way they were opposites.

Maxine met Jim at a concert. She rarely went to church, but that night she had gone to the First Presbyterian Church in Concordia, Kansas, at the request of a friend. The College of Emporia Glee Club was performing, and many of its members, Jim included, were seeking dates.

Jim saw Max in the audience and fell for her immediately. During the performance he pointed her out to a friend and insisted that this was the girl he would marry. Max recalls: "As soon as the service was over I went to the foyer to await the arrival of the glee club. Soon, this very handsome young man came running up to me, offered his hand and said, 'Hi, my name is Jim Rayburn, what's yours?' There was something in his style that swept me off my feet. He was warm, friendly, and confident. We spent the rest of the evening in a little cafe, eating peanuts, drinking Coke, and talking. The next morning Jim picked me up in a taxi and took me to school. You can't imagine the reaction of my classmates when I showed up in a taxi cab."

On this cold, seemingly uneventful night in Concordia, Kansas, Maxine found her prince. She was a senior in high school, Jim a sophomore at the College of Emporia. The date was January 13, 1929; Max was sixteen days shy of her eighteenth birthday.

The young couple wasted no time arranging to study together that Fall at Kansas State University. Maxine, a talented artist, had hoped to pursue a major in art. To pacify her father, however, who thought all artists were bums, she selected home economics as her major.

University life was good for both. Max was a member of the Tri Delta sorority, Jim the Pi Kappa Alpha fraternity. They had each other, they were busy, and life was good. Max was elected the campus beauty queen her freshman year, a tremendous affirmation for a girl with a shattered self-image.

Jim was dating the prettiest girl on campus and was proud as a peacock. He was soon elected president of his fraternity. His parents, who thought that fraternities were educational organiza-

tions, were proud that their son had received such an honor. Little did they know what another world he had entered.

A year earlier, at the College of Emporia, Jim had decided to play football. It didn't go so well. He was rugged and could hold his own on a mountain trail with a goat, but contact sports were not his forte. As he later summed up his football career, "I was fed to the varsity four times a week. They made hamburger out of me almost every practice. Many are the times I awoke in the shower."

Not one to be dismayed, Jim usually found another way to go if his original plans faltered. Since his football career was a washout, he decided to try cheer leading at Kansas State. He made

Helen Maxine Stanley, Kansas State University beauty queen, 1930.

it, too. So at every sporting event that came along, Jim led the troops and directed the band.

These were the Depression years and times were hard. Due to financial shortages, Max was unable to return for her sophomore year. She went back to her stepmother's house in Concordia, and

7

Jim returned to the university to complete his studies. They were together whenever possible.

Upon graduation, Jim headed for a summer of study at the University of Colorado in Boulder. While he was there, a fraternity brother phoned to inform him that Max had been seen with another man. Jim had a mortal fear of losing her, and this was no small threat. As soon as school was out, he headed home and went straight to pick her up. On September 11, 1932, before a justice of the peace in Harrisonville, Missouri, they married.

In Jim's mind, eloping would hold Maxine while he figured out how to manage his parents. He had several problems with which to contend. In the first place, he was scared to death of his folks. Second, by eloping he had smeared the family name and insulted God Almighty, as they were later to inform him. Further, Max was not the kind of girl the Rayburn family held in the highest regard. The four Rayburn boys were expected to choose their wives from the nearest chapter of the Women's Christian Temperance Union, or something similar. Max hardly fit the mold. In the Rayburns' eyes, she may as well have been raised by wolves.

There was another problem, a different kind of problem that no one could see. A few days before marrying Maxine, Jim had offered his life to God. Jim had no idea what this might mean, and Max didn't grasp it either when he told her, sometime after the wedding ceremony in Harrisonville. Jim remembered his commitment like this:

> Out of engineering school, I went to graduate school at Colorado University to specialize in mineralogy. While I was up there I got miserable, like lots of Christians who've been out of touch with the Lord do. One of the things the Lord used to bring me back to myself was a sense of futility and misery. Often I was spending as high as eighteen hours a day in the mineralogy lab, just because I loved to monkey around with rocks. Yet I was unhappy way down deep. Well, I went up on a mountain one night and told the Lord I was sick and tired of the mess I'd made of my life. If He wanted to take over, He could do so. I did the best I knew, in my stumbling way, to take hands off. Believe me, when anybody does that, I don't

care how stumbling and blundering they are, the Lord will take them up on it!

All alone on a mountainside in Boulder, Colorado, a young man cried out to his heavenly Father, made an offering of his life, and unknowingly set in motion a revolution in the course of twentieth-century Christianity. But in 1932, neither Jim nor Maxine realized what had taken place.

Standing before the justice of the peace, Max had no idea that Jim would take her back to Concordia. She had finally married her prince, only to find he wasn't taking her away. Greatly depressed by this turn of events, she returned to her job and waited for Jim to inform his folks. She was doubtful that he would. Ever since her mother left her, Max had struggled with a pessimistic outlook. It was hard for her to believe that anyone would love her permanently. But Jim was always positive and upbeat. Two months after their secret wedding, he wrote:

Maxie, my darling,

I've tried so often to encourage you, both by letter and in person. On almost every occasion I've met with such failure that I hesitate to make the attempt again. But I shall make one more attempt at showing you the bright side of this gloomy situation, despite past failures, and I shall make every promise that is humanly possible regarding our future.

Oh, Maxie, my precious little wife, how my heart has gone out for you since your last two letters arrived. I'd have given a million dollars to have been there when your folks were indulging in all the criticism and thoughtless, inexcusable kidding. Oh, honey, I know it was hard for you. I long to be near you Maxie, and fight your battles for you, and let your heartaches be my heartaches too, as they always are.

Today your letter is full of the blues, worrying about having your job after Christmas. Honey, you won't need your job after Christmas. You don't have to worry about getting fired; you're going to quit. Darling, you're going to be with me! Now, my precious, does the job amount to anything?

I have decided to wait until this series of meetings is over to tell Dad. He needs me badly here and might consider it a most inopportune time to announce a secret marriage. You see, I don't know his viewpoint, and I can't discern it, so this is my only course to safeguard his work and insure my present usefulness to him. So, dear kid, these meetings will close two weeks from next Monday. Immediately thereafter I shall "blow the works" to fond parents. You better have your ear close to the phone to get the outcome right from "ringside." It is going to be the hardest job of my life. I don't know how I'll do it, but I will, don't ever doubt that. I've got to utterly destroy the folks' confidence in me and build it back again, all in the same session.

Now, honey-mine, just think, very soon I'll have you and you'll have me. Honestly darling, no sacrifice would seem great, or nothing hard to give up, if I can have you near me and make you happy. It may be hard, dear, it may be a fight to exist for a while, but we'll have each other and we'll be fighting side by side. Come what may, we'll have our love and we'll have God ever near us. Honey, isn't that enough to make you glad you're alive, anxious to live, and happy, in spite of any trials you are put to?

Now, sweet kid, I want you to be happy. We belong to each other, and the rest of the world can go hang to a sour apple tree. I love you, Maxie. Nothing else matters. So, my sweet baby, just consider yourself forever loved, and stop worrying.

Your own,
"Jimmie," forever

Two weeks later Jim broke the news to his folks. It was not well received. They somehow believed that Max and Jim were "living in sin." Arrangements were hastily made for another wedding ceremony, to be held in the Rayburn home. The day after Christmas, 1932, the young lovers were married for the second time. Max thought the whole thing ridiculous, but Jim was still very much under his parents' authority, and their word was usually final.

Right after Christmas, Jim's father held a series of evangelistic meetings in Seminole, Oklahoma. Jim had planned to take Maxine along on the six-week trip as sort of a belated honeymoon. He had told her his plans, and she was looking forward to the time with her new husband. But unfortunately for Jim and Max, his folks decided she should stay behind and run the household, allowing mother Rayburn to take the trip. Maxine had spent four days with her prince and then he hit the road.

For the next fourteen months the newlyweds stayed at the Rayburn home in Newton, Kansas. Jim was usually on the road assisting his father; Max stayed behind to help her mother-in-law.

Maxine had little church training in her formative years, and she was somewhat self-conscious about it. She looked upon Jim's folks as the "gurus" of all matters spiritual. Naturally, she wanted to learn what she could from them. Almost overnight she found herself in every church service, Women's Christian Temperance Union meeting, Bible study, prayer meeting, and Sunday school class that was scheduled.

In spite of her lack of formal church training, Maxine was a sensitive and loving type who would freely spend her last nickel to feed a hungry cat. Full of generosity and helpfulness toward anyone in trouble or with a need, young Max was refreshingly simple and genuine. She wore no masks, and she accepted most people. Now she found herself in a situation where love was constantly discussed, but infrequently shown. She was taught to call it "the Christian life."

In those tough Depression years many were suffering. One day a hobo called at the Rayburn home. Maxine ran to the door, opened it wide, and was momentarily stunned; in front of her was a cold, thin man with unshaven face, feet wrapped with burlap bags, his deep sunken eyes staring into hers. He hadn't eaten in days, was desperately hungry, and was looking for work. Inviting the man to sit down and wait, Max ran to the bedroom and found a pair of Jim's shoes, tucked them under her arm and headed for the kitchen. She hastily prepared sandwiches, grabbed an apple, and returned to the living room.

As the old man departed and Maxine closed the door behind him, Mother Rayburn made her entrance, exclaiming, "Oh, Maxine, he didn't deserve a thing from us! Didn't you see he was sucking on a cigarette?"

Maxine would struggle for years to understand such incidents. "If a person has love in his heart," she reasoned, "how can he possibly turn a deaf ear to the suffering of any living creature? How can it possibly be wrong to help somebody? Why do I have to go to boring meetings and sit around with stone-faced religious people? Is this what God is like? Am I really supposed to give a hoot whether or not someone smokes, drinks, or dances? What if I don't care—does that make me evil?" Countless questions flooded her mind. It wasn't easy to find answers, because she looked upon Jim's folks as model Christians. Theirs was the way that led to Christ and salvation, she was told.

Tragically, Jim was unaware of the conflict brewing within his young bride. Although he feared his parents, he didn't take their narrow ways as seriously as she did. He and his brother Paul, for example, were excellent card players, and both were known to pick up spare change utilizing card skills. Card playing was on the top ten sins list in the Rayburn home. There was one exception, however, a game called Rook. The two brothers developed a way to play bridge with Rook cards. Telling their mother they had invented a new, more exciting version of Rook, they taught her to play bridge. She loved the game so much she told people all over town about it. She even gave lessons to the other women in her various church groups. Soon, the whole church was playing bridge (and loving it!).

Unfortunately, Max didn't have the ability to make a game of all the legalism; it really confused her. At the point in her life when she was eager to know of Christ, she was handed a set of rules and regulations. Little emphasis was put on inward growth, only externals mattered.

Maxine was not by nature a narrow-minded, legalistic person, but she lacked the strength to follow her own intuitions. Faced with this new, religious way of approaching life, she was unable to argue against it, as she knew very little about the Bible, Jesus Christ, churches, or church people.

Although Jim was unaware of Max's deep inner conflict, he could see she wasn't very happy. In February of 1934, he was offered a job with the Presbyterian Board of National Missions in New Mexico. The young couple saw this as an opportunity to start their life anew, away from parents and in-laws. In March, they enthusiastically accepted the job and headed for the great Southwest.

Country Pastor

CHAMA, New Mexico, was Jim's kind of place, but to Maxine it felt like the outer limit of civilization. Max had never been a robust, outdoor type of person. She wasn't one to pioneer new territory or blaze a new trail. Jim, on the other hand, was constantly on the lookout for a new adventure. A wild and remote place like Chama was just his type of playground.

There was one Protestant church in Rio Arriba County; Jim was the pastor. Behind the church was the manse, a dilapidated wooden structure which served as home. It looked like something from a ghost town, lacking wiring as well as indoor plumbing. The "bathroom" was a fine two-seater outhouse a short walk away, which also served as the church rest room.

The former pastor had made no splash in the community and attendance at his church was minimal. The solution, Jim figured, was to personally call on everyone in the county. Life became a daily routine of trips into remote areas of northern New Mexico in search of any miners, ranchers, Indians, or others who might live there. Usually Max went along. If they could drive, they did; if there were no adequate roads, travel was by foot or on horseback. They slept in the car, on the mountainsides, and inside rat-infested buildings with dirt floors. Jim felt he was serving the Lord and enthusiastically accepted the challenges, but his wife found the routine difficult beyond anything she'd ever imagined.

Max had never wanted to be a preacher's wife; that role didn't mesh with her personality. As Jim's degree in civil engineering had not opened any doors to employment, however, he had accepted this job as a means of leaving Kansas. The way Max viewed it, living in New Mexico would at least provide them with more time together. It didn't pan out. If Max wanted to be with Jim she had to accompany him, something she had neither the physical strength nor emotional grit to continue. She began to spend more time at home while Jim pursued his visitations, but the seeds of discontentment over Jim's increasing absence had taken root.

Being one of four sons, little did Jim realize how Max needed him. He had spent little time around women and was somewhat naïve about his wife's emotional needs. The only woman he had real exposure to was his mother, who gladly kept the home fires burning while his father was away preaching. Jim was simply following in his father's footsteps, and that's precisely what concerned Maxine.

One early spring morning Jim was returning from another excursion. Eager to get home, he was pushing the speedometer a bit, as was his custom. On the roadway ahead he noticed a car stopped on the shoulder and group of people looking it over. Pulling to his left to allow more room for passing, Jim slowed his car as he approached. Without warning, an elderly man wandered from behind the stalled car directly onto the highway. There was no time to swerve. Jim heard the sound of screeching tires interrupted by the awful impact he was hoping to avoid.

As Jim's vehicle came to a stop, he could hear the screams of the people behind him. Shaking, he ran to the broken, bloodied body lying by the roadside. Jim knelt down and took the old man in his arms. He was still alive! Blinking back tears, Jim struggled to his feet with the injured man in his arms and carried him to the car. From the accident scene to the doctor's house was both the fastest and the longest drive of Jim's life—all to no avail. The old man died before they arrived.

Outside of Maxine, Jim never told anyone about the accident, an event that undeniably affected his image in the area. Four of the old man's relatives came to the house a week later and threatened to even the score. Several very tense weeks followed and Jim's ministry in Chama, so enthusiastically begun, died by the roadside. Seven months later, in January of 1935, the Board of Missions moved the young couple to Douglas, Arizona, a small town on the Mexican border.

Jim arrived in Douglas determined to reach out and meet everyone in southern Arizona, just as he'd done in northern New Mexico. Once again, his life became a daily routine of scouting out the territory. Jim's January 29, 1935 journal:

> Maxine's birthday—got her a little perfume. She and I spent the whole day traveling over field. Visited McNeal, where I spoke in school, also went to schools at Whitewater, Webb, Ash Creek, and Sunglow. All worth investigating. McNeal and Sunglow seem best prospects. No work at either of these. Feeling rather low tonight. Contacts today not as enthusiastic as I had hoped.

> February 1, 1935: Maxine and I left home about 8:30, drove to Gleeson. I went to the school but got "no house." Sunday school superintendent not at home. Drove on to Tombstone and took "short-cut" to Dragoon. What a trip! Cow-trails part of the way. Stopped at Birch's ranch house midway. Wonderful country up in the forest reserve. Met young Adams, horseback. Would like to look this country over. Stopped at Dragoon school. Mostly Mexican children. Drove into Texas. Had supper at Lays. Drove home.

As in Chama, Maxine found the pace too frantic, the comforts too few, and her motivation lacking. Jim, on the other hand, would always go the extra mile. His official duty was to pastor the local church and establish a program for the youngsters. Concerning his Sunday school, the first thing he attempted, Jim would later say, "If you want anybody to show up, don't have it on Sunday and don't call it school." At first it surprised him that most kids wanted no part of Sunday school. Disliking it had not been an option for

15

Jim. The path of least resistance had been to accept the many hours spent in church; Jim had never realized that kids almost hated it. As soon as he caught on, Jim shifted the emphasis of his work to activities well outside his church building. In no time, he and Max were up to their eyebrows in Cub Scout meetings, Boy Scout meetings, and camping trips.

Having grown up in a stifling religious environment where most people were less than honest, Jim was immensely attracted to open-minded, sincere people. Because they usually possess these qualities, teenage people were very special to him. Further, no group of people is more enthusiastic about life and living than high school kids. Jim was the only adult most kids knew who shared this enthusiasm. Teenagers, even if they didn't understand most adults, had little trouble understanding Jim; he was a live wire, full of youthful enthusiasm.

Jim soon found a secret to successful work with kids—simply include them in the activities he'd long enjoyed, crossing the boundary of age with the offer of true friendship—a simple, and basic concept. For hundreds of young people in southern Arizona, that meant outdoor camping. While seated around an open fire, gazing into the glorious Arizona night sky, and listening to the nearby stream, Jim would share his thoughts on what really matters in life. His manner of speaking was wonderfully fresh. The longer he talked, the more his listeners paid attention—an uncommon reversal of the norm.

In a kind of cute and endearing way Jim would dare his young listeners to take him seriously. With that slow, Jimmy Stewart type of drawl, he would warmly challenge, "Now if you think you've got something more important to think about than Jesus Christ, then you just come over here and put your little nose up against mine and tell little old Jim what you think is more important." He seldom had any takers. By the time he sent the kids off to bed down, most of them were in pretty deep thought. It was usually the first time these kids had ever thought about the subject, too, as most were long-time dropouts from anything with spiritual or religious overtones. They hadn't come into the woods to seek God either, but Jim didn't look or act religious, and what he had to say was interesting. He was much more like a friend, or big brother.

Jim truly enjoyed his work with kids, but found pastoring a church was not his call. He abhorred the idea of being called "Reverend," and would not permit people to so address him. The pastor's image in Jim's mind was of one who acted above we mortals—one who preached long, dull sermons, and prayed long, dull prayers, usually in a verbose and pompous style. Jim just didn't fit that mold; he had a warm and sincere concern for others, a zest for life, and a sense of humor that worked overtime.

"I remember a time when Jim overheard some negative talk about the local Douglas, Arizona, bum," Maxine recalled. "Well, the first thing Jim did was to look up that lonely old man and issue him a warm and special invitation to our home. Jim really had a heart for people like that—people that no one cared about."

One Sunday morning, Jim was dutifully leading the church service when his new friend, the town drunk, stumbled in the door and slowly shuffled up the aisle to a seat near the pulpit. A few minutes later it was time for the offering. A large tin can that reverberated loudly each time a coin was dropped into it served as the offering plate. When it came to the drunk, he reached into his pocket and took out ten silver dollars, raised his hand high in the air, and dropped each one individually into the can. After this lengthy ritual of clang-clang-clang, the old boy staggered to his feet and slowly made his way up the aisle, never to return again.

From that point on, when Jim needed money for his trips with the kids, that same town drunk financed his projects. Whether the need was food, sleeping bags, gasoline, or tents, the local drunk provided. The "Christian" community had treated the man with either apathy or contempt for many years, but it had never treated him with love. Jim simply offered his friendship to a lonely old man, and God opened up a most unexpected source of financial supply. With God as his guide, Maxine as his assistant, and the town drunk providing the resources, Jim's work with kids was off and running.

The last church Jim and Max would tackle was in Clifton, Arizona, a small copper mining town several hours north of Douglas. While passing through Clifton in October of 1935, a year before their move, Maxine had commented that she wouldn't be caught dead there. It was not a scenic place. "In the process of scouting out the territory," Maxine recalled, "Jim had met some wonderful people in Clifton who begged him to move there and work with the town's young people. Further, their little mission church had been without a pastor for some time, and they wanted Jim to take it on. I went with what I'd call 'cheerful acceptance' of the situation. I wanted to be with Jim—if that meant Siberia, then I'd have gone there."

Home in Clifton was a decrepit old wooden manse with no luxuries, save for the small library. One night, while Max was at the movie theater, Jim discovered an old coverless copy of a book that would change his life. The book, *He That Is Spiritual*, taught about the Holy Spirit, Grace, and Salvation. Jim had never understood these subjects as Chafer presented them.

1937 - Home in Clifton, AZ. The Manse

"How misleading is the theory," Chafer wrote, "that to be spiritual one must abandon play, diversion, and helpful amusement. Such a conception is born of a morbid human conscience. It is foreign to the Word of God. It is a device of Satan to make the blessings of God seem abhorrent to people who are overflowing with physical life and energy. There are many who in blindness are emphasizing negatives, giving the impression that spirituality is opposed to joy, liberty, and naturalness of expression. True spirituality is not a pious pose. It is not a 'Thou shall not,' it is a 'Thou shalt.' We cannot be normal physically, mentally, or spiritually if we neglect this vital factor in human life. God has provided that our joy shall be full."

Jim had never read anything like that before. His early diaries frequently mention that he spoke to this group, or that, on the evils of dancing. Other taboos against alcohol, games, cigarettes, movies, make-up, playing cards, and so on, had been spoon-fed to him since birth. His parents' influence had been enormous. Had not the town drunk helped him most, however? Which was The Way? Chafer's book intensified the struggle. What Jim was reading was speaking to his heart like a beautiful melody, but it challenged everything he'd been raised to believe.

Although Jim had resisted many of the narrow teachings he'd received as a child, he had never been freed from the guilt of questioning the religious status quo. As he read Chafer he could hardly contain his excitement. Years later he would tell about his momentous discovery of salvation by grace:

> I was a gospel preacher, I led people to the Lord Jesus Christ, I was a member of the Board of National Missions of the Presbyterian Church, if you please, before I ever heard of this—the absolute finality and perfection of what Jesus Christ has done about sin.
>
> All my life I ran scared. I remember five years in engineering school and graduate school in geology, when all I did about my Christian life was occasionally pray, "Now I lay me down to sleep, I pray the Lord my soul to keep." A great big, strapping boy, a college man, praying baby prayers.

I fooled around and left out the Lord, and all that time I was uncomfortable about sin. I never could get into it like my friends at the fraternity house. Oh, I had some minor pleasures here and there, but I was always troubled about this sin business. "Sin . . . golly, I gotta pay for these sins." Do you ever think that? Get way down deep in your insides where you're alone with yourself and God, and you know you think, "Golly, a person as fouled up as I am is gonna have to pay." Well, you're not! It's been paid for.

My thinking may have never changed had not, by the divine providence of God, I come in contact with the inimitable Dr. Chafer, the greatest teacher that I know of or have read of, about the doctrine of the grace of God, who Jesus Christ is, and what Jesus Christ has done.

I don't care if you start with the New Testament, or if you take the Apostles' Creed ,or the Nicene Creed, or the Thirty-nine Articles, or what you take. Every single creed says, "Salvation is something that God did by Himself, and we can't do anything about it." It's a package that's all wrapped up and delivered! And I know very well that most Christians don't know that, and don't believe it if they've heard it. And you know that sometimes you have some doubts about it yourself.

We don't believe in the Roman ideas of going up the steps of the cathedral on our knees, or rubbing our nose down a 300-foot aisle that's full of dust, but we do believe that if we're really going to be saved, then we're going to have to pull up our socks and get going, keeping a bunch of rules. And every time we do that, we get the human element into the perfection of what Jesus Christ has already done. Christ did not free us to practice religion, He freed us from religion.

Thus far, Jim's awareness of his work had been limited to a sense of doing the right thing to the best of his knowledge. He conscientiously went through the motions required by a demanding task. His youthful zeal not withstanding, he was very much on his own. What he lacked, as he came to look back upon this period, was a sense of the Presence of God. He said he "Didn't know the Lord in a very special way and didn't know what to talk to people about. So I talked to them about what they did, more than I talked to them about the Lord." But all of that started to change one night in the fall of 1935 as he read from the pages of a dusty old book.

Jim's diary of November eighth simply records 'some interesting reading on *spirituality*.' "Jim didn't write much in his journal about the impact of Chafer's book upon him," Maxine recalled, "but make no mistake, he was never the same after reading it. He frequently read portions of it to me, and he talked about it daily. It not only whetted his appetite for further study, and pointed him in the direction of a seminary education, but it had a profound effect upon his own relationship with the Lord."

As Jim's dear friend, Emile Cailliet, said in his 1964 book *Young Life*, "Strange, how a dusty old coverless book had spoken straight to Jim's heart one dark and quiet night as he read by the light of a candle. And as he bent over the poorly lit pages, the Spirit of Life was contending with him—no longer as an abstract doctrine, no longer as an *it* , but as He who bears witness to Christ in the soul. And as the light of that candle faded away in the dawn of a new day, Jim knew the great Seeker had found him. Jim was endued and the Spirit was clothed."

Seminary

CHAPTER 4

THERE was a new fire in Jim's spirit, a fresh soaring in his soul, a freedom he had never known before. He was coming to understand that God truly loved him, and had accepted him, warts and all. His salvation was no longer a matter of self effort, keeping rules, and going to church. Salvation was something God had already wrapped up and delivered. Jim could accept it, or reject it, but outside of those two options he had no role to play. Salvation was certainly not something he could earn. It is the ultimate gift from God to all men who come to the end of themselves. No one deserves it, and no one can earn it. To Jim, this was a whole new realm of understanding. But what a relief! God was good after all, far better than he had ever imagined.

Aware that he was uneducated in these matters, and having not yet learned that the Holy Spirit would be his teacher, Jim decided to pursue a seminary education. Having come from a line of Calvinists, Jim was excited as he dropped his application to Princeton Seminary in the Clifton, Arizona, mailbox. He and Max proceeded with plans for their move to New Jersey. They weren't concerned about his being accepted, as he had a distinguished academic record in both high school and college, as well as a long list of extracurricular activities on his records.

Finally the long-awaited letter from Princeton arrived. Jim was shocked to read, "Application rejected." The letter explained that Jim wasn't viewed as the proper material to be a Presbyterian minister. The problem, as they viewed it at Princeton, was his heavy interest in the sciences. Years later, this became an embarrassment to the folks at Princeton; one of the school's respected presidents, John A. McKay, would later refer to Jim as one of the great saints of this century.

Having been turned down by Princeton, there were two options left: San Francisco Seminary in California, and Dallas Seminary in Texas. Jim and Max were in a quandary—summer was almost over and classes were starting soon, regardless of the school chosen. With all of their possessions packed, the young couple left the scene of their Arizona labors and soon reached the fork in the highway that branched off east and west. There they stopped the car and prayed, asking God in what direction He would have them turn. They turned east.

The years in the Southwest had been good, although not without struggles and heartache. Jim and Max had lost two children through miscarriage, feared for their lives in Chama, and struggled with the poverty of Depression days. But these years had provided them the opportunity to be together, away from the strict religious environment of Newton, and had given both a chance to breath some 'fresh air.'

Maxine's influence on her husband had been most positive during this period. Living with her was teaching him about love, open-mindedness, and freedoms. When she caught Jim smoking in the shed behind the house, she simply laughed, enabling him to do the same. That was a funny incident, as Jim had confiscated the smokes from his younger brother, after delivering a stern lecture on the evils of tobacco.

In his heart, Jim didn't feel such things were important spiritual issues, but he couldn't step free from the guilt of breaking the many rules learned in church. He smoked his whole life, but never felt the freedom to do so in public. In essence, he feared the rejection and judgment of his Christian peers. Some of Jim's attempts to stop smoking were hilarious. He once got motivated to quit while on a horseback ride with a group of friends, found the inspiration, and victoriously tossed his cigarettes away in the brush. They then continued riding an hour or so and stopped for the night to camp. Later that evening, craving a cigarette in the worst way, Jim rode his horse all the way back and spent considerable time looking in the bushes for his smokes.

In late September, 1936, Jim and Max arrived at the Dallas Seminary campus. Maxine was there to be with Jim; he was there to be with L.S. Chafer. Max was excited at the prospect of having her husband home at night, finally.

While the men were in class, the wives had assorted get-togethers. With little else to do, Max made these meetings a regular part of her life. She recalls: "I remember a strong feeling that I didn't fit in. I'd look around and see the conservative dresses, the ugly shoes, and the missionary hairstyles, and I stuck out like a black sheep. Well, I didn't like dressing that way at all, but I guess I felt these women were right. I was just a 'babe' in Christ, and most of them were long-time church members. After a while I started to imitate them. I wasn't conscious of it at the time, but in looking back I feel that I was losing my identity. I was trying to emulate people that I didn't agree with in my heart. I hadn't considered that the atmosphere of a seminary just wasn't fertile soil for me."

Occasionally Max would go with Jim to his theology class, taught by Chafer. She learned much from this experience, but didn't know how to relate his input with that of others. Many people at the seminary talked far more about sin than about grace. Says Maxine: "I had never been

Maxine at Dallas Theological Seminary, trying to look, dress and act in the proper way, a way she loathed deep within. She too was getting starched and ironed before being washed. Her problems had begun.

exposed to people who talked about sin all the time. I guess my concept of sin was vastly different from theirs, but I had so little confidence in my own feelings. As I had done with Jim's family, I figured that these people knew more than I, so I was quite open to their teaching me what Christ was all about. So many things were considered evil that I just stopped living. That's when I started to wrestle with depression."

After the first year of studies, Jim committed himself to a summer job in Arizona. In her fourth month of pregnancy, Max was most reluctant to see him leave, but going with him was out of the question. Having had two miscarriages, she was concerned that she might have a third and she had no desire to face it alone. Jobs were few and far between, however, and Jim felt he had no other option; Maxine disagreed.

She had married Jim to be with him, believing that his only desire was to be with her, and she had no desire to face life's problems without her man close by her side. Ironically, Jim needed a strong woman who could keep the wagons rolling while he was up ahead scouting out the territory. After much debate, Jim headed for the country to lead summer youth camps, and Max stayed behind in the seminary apartment.

Several weeks later Max saw a Western Union delivery boy on campus and deeply sensed he had a message for her. She was right. A telegram informed her that Jim was in an Albuquerque hospital. His appendix had ruptured, gangrene had developed, and his life was hanging in the balance.

Under severe emotional stress, Max called her doctor. He made it clear that her odds of avoiding another miscarriage were fifty-fifty if she stayed put, but he gave her no chance of having the baby if she traveled. Max desperately wished to be with her dying husband, but she didn't want to lose their baby. There was no other solution, she finally reasoned, than to stay where she was and pray for Jim's recovery. But with her husband hanging to life by a thread, anxiety and despondency waged war on Maxine's spirit. She was gripped by fear: fear of losing her husband, her baby, or both, fear of having to face life by herself, and fear of her deteriorating emotions.

Jim's condition was critical. He had developed peritonitis, a fecal fistula, and abdominal gangrene. As there were no antibiotics in those days, his recovery was viewed as an impossibility. The foul odor of gangrene permeated his room so the hospital staff moved Jim's bed to the doorway with his head in the hall. They draped a sheet from the top of the door casing down over his chest to provide an odor barrier. For thirty-five days Jim lingered in this hopeless condition while the hospital staff awaited his death.

After weeks of wasting away, Jim miraculously improved. His doctors were shocked, simply calling it a miracle, something they couldn't explain. When Jim insisted that he must return home, the doctors reluctantly gave him permission to take the train back to Dallas. Maxine was only weeks away from delivering their first baby, and there was no way Jim would stay away if he had strength to walk.

Maxine remembered his arrival, "I met him at the train station, and I was so excited to have him back! I wasn't prepared for the shock, however. It was a walking corpse that stepped off that train. He had jaundice, so his color was awful, and he had lost about forty pounds. He was very thin, very weak, and still had an awful open wound in his abdomen. For several weeks I was pretty sure he wouldn't survive."

It didn't take long and Jim was continuing his studies. Sometimes, after class, he was taken to the Baylor Medical College as an exhibit for the medical students. The doctors of Dallas and Albuquerque were all amazed that he recovered. In these days, people didn't develop gangrene in the abdomen and live—not without antibiotics.

On October 17, 1937, Max gave birth to their first child, Elna Ann. The parents were proud and the baby was healthy. All the tensions and uncertainties of the previous months had culminated in a peaceful and normal delivery. Things seemed on the upswing for Jim and Max after a dreadfully stressful summer. But it was not to be.

"They kept you in the hospital for ten days back then," Maxine recalled. "I remember coming home with the baby and feeling like something was wrong with me. Jim was studying, our baby was sleeping, and I was resting on the bed. It hit me that I had never been around a baby and didn't know how to care for one. Also, Jim's

Ann Rayburn, the couple's first child.

recovery had been slow, and I was still afraid his condition might worsen.

"But mainly, I felt the environment of the seminary was gloomy, and I didn't want to be there any longer. I was overcome with fear and depression. It was far worse than I can describe, like an emotional black hole. Suddenly, something snapped and I started to weep uncontrollably. I had trouble breathing and was overcome with a feeling of utter panic. It was the worst experience I'd ever been through."

It would not be hard to believe that Jim and Maxine were under attack by an unseen enemy. After Jim recovered from abdominal gangrene the attack was targeted more directly upon Maxine. This side of heaven, no one will ever fully know what was going on here. But Jim and Maxine couldn't buy a break when it came to the subject of emotional and physical health. The doctors simply diagnosed Maxine's trauma as a 'nervous breakdown.'

Whether a nervous breakdown or something more defined, Maxine was not the same. Years later, she came to understand that the main cause of her distress was her loss of interest in life itself. She explained, "There's a song that says, 'If you want joy, real joy, wonderful joy, let Jesus come into your heart.' As I viewed the world around me, I saw so very few people who had anything I'd call joy. Most of the people at seminary were singing about a joy I couldn't see they possessed. To me, it was like a big masquerade party, with everybody wearing a mask.

"I was so tired of fighting the current, I loved to dance but dancing was considered sinful, so I quit. I had always paid attention to my appearance, but makeup and hemlines were such big issues that I quit trying to look nice. I had always been a non judgmental type, but I found myself adopting the very same attitudes that I had always disagreed with. That's when my problem with weight began. Almost everything I was interested in was looked down upon, or considered sinful.

"Now I see that as I quit being myself, my depression intensified. Jim's illness and my fears about motherhood were true concerns, but the major problem was—I was losing touch with the real Maxine. The thing Christ desired for me was the freedom to be myself, so He could live out His life in me unrestrained, but I didn't know that then, and no one was telling me about it."

Max exemplifies countless people weighed down by a false message that Christ never taught. The Gospel of Jesus Christ is not an adherence to conservative codes of dress and conduct. It is not a religious exercise wherein the Christian is expected to keep a set of rules and regulations. Those who were bound by an adherence to conservative codes of conduct, the apostle Paul referred to as "false brothers who had sneaked into the body of believers to spy out the liberty of those who followed Christ." Paul went on to say that their purpose was to bring us back into religious bondage.

This bondage, codes of dress and conduct, is known as legalism. Sadly, "Christianity" has been infected with legalism since the first century, and it has created a counterfeit faith that's accepted as the real thing by multitudes.

Human beings are natural, born legalists. We all tend to see morality externally. But God looks within, in our hearts. For example, over the years most "Christians" have made a big issue over things like smoking and drinking alcoholic beverages, as though that has something to do with following the Lord. But Jesus taught that it's not what goes into our mouth that's the problem, but rather what comes out (the hurtful things we say, the ugly things we talk about, gossip, being judgmental, etc.). When the light begins to dawn that this external goodness is just a mask that conceals an unloving, me first, self-righteous heart, it is then that we stand on the precipice of receiving the very Spirit of God into our lives. Seeing our own hypocrisy is the problem; we can see our neighbor's but not our own. If we make it, we usually shed some big tears over what we find inside ourselves.

"The sacrifices of God are a broken spirit: a broken and a contrite heart, O God, Thou will not despise" (Psalm 51:17). It's a shock, and a heartbreak, to see ourselves as we are, but that is the key to the kingdom—a broken, contrite heart. Give those tears to God and he will give you a wonderful, wonderful treasure—a new heart, a kind heart, a loving heart, and a freedom from rules and regulations. Anyone who comes to Him, helpless and hopeless, He will make into a new creation. That's what being "born again" is all about.

Nothing closes the door of our hearts to God's Spirit so effectively as the religious observance of rules, regulations, and codes of conduct. Ironically, as Dr. Chafer was liberating Jim from the legalism of his past, some of the seminary women were pushing Maxine towards the "legalistic quicksand."

Jim had no understanding of Maxine's deteriorating emotions. He was accustomed to conservative religious environments and found the seminary atmosphere rather liberal if compared to his past. He was learning from L.S. Chafer about the Holy Spirit, and his head was swimming with exciting new revelations. But while Jim's spiritual sensitivities were growing like a young bear cub, Maxine's had gone into hibernation.

Young Life

DURING the 1938-39 school year, Jim decided to take a part-time job with a Gainesville, Texas, church. Jim was the assistant pastor in charge of young people; Clyde Kennedy, a minister with progressive ideas, was his boss.

Together the two men hashed out a novel idea—that Jim would work with unchurched kids exclusively, instead of with those who already attended. Nothing suited Jim better than this approach. Experiences in the Southwest had taught him that most high school kids avoid church if given a choice. Besides, Jim wasn't fond of titles such as "minister," "youth-worker," or "pastor," and he had a real aversion to black robes, clerical collars, and religious garb.

Armed with a soft spot in his heart for kids, and a burning love affair with God, Jim headed for the local high school. Little did anyone suspect how far-reaching his efforts would be.

Jim studied every available book on youth ministries, yet failed to run across anything with which he agreed. Through Clyde Kennedy, his path crossed that of a Mrs. McClusky, a lady who was also working with high school students; she and her club hostesses called their group the "Miracle Book Club." Maxine recalled, "Jim liked that name and wanted to adopt it for his own work. Unfortunately, adopting the name meant adopting Mrs. McClusky and her chapter hostesses." At first, progress was slow and results were disappointing. Meeting once a week after school in an empty class-room, Jim managed to interest eleven kids. For a man who loved to think big, this was a major disappointment; his "Miracle Book Club" was working no miracle. Jim recalled:

> *I didn't know how to run a club. I started having it in the afternoon, after school. I'd talked the school people into giving me a classroom. I started with three kids. One of them turned out to be a Christian, and the other two didn't turn out to be anything. They just faded out. I got it up as high as eleven that year, but I'm telling you, it was the saddest bunch of sacks you every saw in your life.*
>
> *If you want to really see a bunch of sad apples, just have a meeting for the kids who'll stay after school. I got the biggest selection of teachers' pets you ever saw, not a red corpuscle in the whole crowd. Everybody I wanted to reach was out on the football field, and every place else, right while we were having our club meeting. After nine months of that, I knew I had to try something else.*

Jim would later say about this time period,

> *I didn't know what I was doing but at least I was doing a lot. I had a Good News Club out by the Ford factory and I had a Young People's Fellowship over at West Minster Presbyterian Church and I had a Miracle Book Club out at another place and I just had everything. All of it was work with kids though and the Lord just seemed in many different ways to direct me to young-sters, from the very first time I got out on the mission field, out in Chama, New Mexico and other places I saw how hard nosed and set in their ways adults were. While they needed spiritual inspiration they didn't respond to it. They weren't going to do anything about the Lord. The kids were though.*
>
> *I'd take kids on a camping trip and share the Gospel with them around a campfire a few nights and some of them would close in with the Lord. That always happened. Never failed. That's what always appealed to me about kids work and that's the reason I don't understand why the church goes on like an ostrich with its head in the sand, spending 99.5 percent of its*

energy and time and talent and money on the old folks who have heard the message all their life and just let the kids work go to grass. Aunt Sadie Glutz or any dear willing soul who wants the high school department can have it. That's just wrong.

A short time later, in January of 1940, Jim changed the Miracle Book Club format. The hour was changed from after school to early evening. And as kids preferred out-of-school activities, the meetings were moved into the homes of various students.

Jim and Maxine's second child, Mary Margaret, was born March 13, 1940, just as the Miracle Book Club was really starting to roll. Jim's diaries mix gratitude for a healthy wife and child with praise for increased attendance at club meetings:

3/11/1940: *Fifty-five at Miracle Book Club at Brodheads tonight—a truly wonderful meeting. Seven made a public confession of Christ as Savior: "Burr" Nichols, football captain, "Bud" Teage, "Tippy" Marshall, Ann Culp and Carrie Lou Lindell amongst them—That makes nineteen who have testified to salvation in the past 4 weeks! 102 on the Miracle Book Club roll.*

3/13: *Our little "Mary Margaret" was born at 7:15 p.m. I took Maxine to the hospital about 3:30—she had considerable pain but this was nothing compared to last time. Praise the Lord for this wonderful gift of his love and the high privilege of being entrusted with another little life.*

3/18: *Eighty-two at Miracle Book Club tonight. The greatest attendance ever and a wonderful meeting. Truly the Lord is answering our prayers in a wonderful way. He is the Faithful One!*

4/1: *One-hundred at Miracle Book club tonight—What a club— what a victory the Lord has wrought—most amazing to see all the worldly and otherwise indifferent to the Gospel youngsters that came.*

In a message given years later, Jim reminisced about this period, and the wonderful results achieved when he moved his meetings from afternoons to evenings, and into the private homes of students:

What a change! I started having lively meetings. Two or three kids came out who were really sharp and could do something with the rest of the bunch. Their personal enthusiasm for the club got others to come, and it was wonderful. Right at the start the Lord got hold of two kids. One of them was Viddie Murphy. She was the very first youngster that was ever led to the Lord Jesus Christ in a club of mine. She was in with that little high school society set, and she got those kids to come to club, she and a boy in the senior class.

We decided we'd have a prayer meeting, those two kids and me. In the pastor's study that Sunday night, we started to pray for the club. The pastor met with us. He was pushing on me all the time. He didn't care if I did any work around the church. He just wanted to see those kids reached for Christ. He said, "Don't monkey around with the people who come to church. I'll take care of them. You go on down to that high school." Boy, now just think of that. I wonder what would happen if there were more pastors like that, if there were some pastors in every town like that. That just said, "Boy, I'm not doing so bad with the people who are coming to church. The thing that's bothering me is all those people who don't come. Somebody go out and get them." That's what the church is all about, really.

You can't read the book of Acts, you can't read the New Testament, you can't read of the life and ministry of Jesus Christ, without coming to the conclusion that that's what the church is here for, to go after others. And why it's such a colossal flop is because it's so ingrown. Nobody hears the message except those who have always heard it, and they're not going to do anything about it, so nothing happens. This guy just kept pushing me and pushing me and pushing me, and out I went.

I don't even think the prayer meeting was my idea. We'd had twelve kids at our club meeting the night those two kids came through for the Lord, and we decided to have this prayer meeting, and the next week we had twenty-three. And boy, we had another prayer meeting, a prayer meeting that wouldn't quit. And the next week we had thirty-two. In two weeks we went from twelve to thirty-two. And then we had another prayer meet-

ing, and the school was really out then. The next night we met in the biggest home in the whole town, and we had fifty-one. And right at the end of the meeting, one of the toughest kids in the senior class got up and said, "Wait a minute, I wanted to tell you that I accepted Jesus Christ while Jim was talking." It was like a bomb dropped in the place. None of us had ever heard of anything like that. It was wonderful!

One or two others who had gotten "waked up" joined the prayer meeting the next Sunday night, and from fifty-one we went to sixty-two, and from sixty-two to seventy-five. We had two meetings of seventy-five, and kept praying.

A beautiful little blond girl, the school beauty queen, came to know the Savior and joined in that prayer meeting. She had never been in a prayer meeting in her whole life. We were praying around in a circle, taking turns, and she heard us praying for Burr Nichols, the captain of the football team. As soon as we raised our heads up from prayer, this little blond girl piped up and said, "I'll get Burr." She was going with him, and said she'd bring him to the next meeting. Just like that! That prayer was answered fast!

We started the next meeting, and that night I'll never forget. It was crowded in that hall where we were meeting. It was a big front hall, but seventy-five people are a lot of people for a hall. They were sitting on the floor, and I was crammed up against the front door. I kept looking for this blond girl and Burr Nichols. They weren't there.

We went through the songs, and it was time for my message. I'd stalled as long as I could, and just as I was getting up to speak, there came a clomp, clomp, clomp across the front porch. That door busted open behind me and here was this little blond cutie and Burr Nichols right behind her. She just pranced in and sat down in front of me. That was the only space on the whole floor. And there was Burr standing in front of that whole crowd; he turned around and sunk down beside her.

Well, I started in, and I was scared to death. I was just shaking in my boots. I gave the Gospel the best I knew. Burr hadn't been at the beginning of the meeting, he hadn't heard any singing or anything, but something about it he liked. He came around afterwards and stuck out his big mitt, shook my hand and said, "Boy, Jim, I liked that. I'm coming back next week."

Next week we started off with the same situation—a big crowd jammed up against the front door, but Burr Nichols wasn't there. I went all the way through and came to the message time again. I saw the little blond girl in the audience and thought, "Oh, oh, they've had a divorce this week." But I was wrong.

Just as I started to speak, there came this awful clomp, clomp, clomp across the front porch. Burr opened the front door and came in like he owned the place. He walked past me and said, "Jim, I wouldn't have been so late, but I couldn't find some of these guys." And four teammates came trailing in behind him.

I found out that across the street from the high school a group of elderly women had been meeting for six years, every Monday morning, getting down on their knees in the living room of dear old Mrs. Frasher's. They prayed every Monday morning for six years, long before I ever heard of Gainesville, Texas, for the high school kids across the street. I was there a year before I heard of that prayer meeting. I used to go over there with those five or six old ladies and get down on my knees with them after that club started to roll. That was the thing the Lord used to start it.

Back in seminary, a group of kids going to school there got interested in this club and started to pray. They'd meet every Monday night and pray while I went to the club meeting in Gainesville. They'd get down on their knees and spend hours praying for that club meeting. It's no wonder we had a revival in that school!

That's how Young Life started. I didn't have in my mind to start anything, but that club went from 75 to 96, and then to 100, and then to 119, and 135, and the week before finals there were 170 kids there.

Burr Nichols closed in with the Savior about the fifth night he ever heard the Gospel. That fall Burr went to Dallas to spot players for the announcer at one of their games. Riding back, they had a terrible accident and Burr was killed. His folks wanted me to

*preach the funeral. They said I was the only preacher Burr had
ever listened to.*

*Burr grew up on the wrong side of the tracks and was a
regular ruffian. All the Lord was waiting for was somebody to
get a little bit interested in Burr—a little blond beauty queen and
a little pip-squeak theological student. Burr was a precious soul
for whom the Lord died. This country is full of people like that.
There are thousands of people in this country that no Christian
has ever said a kind word to. Most of the kids in this nation are
like that. A few million more of them will graduate from high
school this year. Just like Burr Nichols, they never heard the
story. And I can't stand that.*

To love-starved young people, Jim sought to be a friend. Kids
listened to Jim when they wouldn't listen to others because they
knew he cared for them. And once he had built a bridge of friendship, he was naturally anxious to share the source of his love. Jim
figured it is best to demonstrate love, kindness, and friendship to
people before confronting them with the issue of their salvation.
He considered this common sense approach as simply what it is—
common sense. But as theologians like labels and doctrines, Jim would
later give it some names: earning the right to be heard, friendship evangelism, and incarnational ministry. Ironically, organized religion found
this approach to be an absolutely novel concept.

In half a year, attendance at Jim's Miracle Book Club had
increased tenfold. Results like these were unheard of in Christian
circles; those who knew of Jim's success with the high school crowd
were awestruck. Many were asking, "How could anyone attract such
numbers of kids to a meeting where the Gospel was presented?" The
very question implies that the life of Jesus Christ isn't interesting, at
least not to teens, but Jim couldn't imagine that anyone who knew
the Gospel would think it dull. He reasoned, therefore, that a person who thinks this way just doesn't know the story. Further, Jim
had already learned that young people are the most open-minded
people in the world. Kids do not bring a head full of staid religious ideas
into a personal encounter with Christ. When Jim talked about his Lord,
no open-minded person thought it dull.

Maxine was not doing well as the seminary days drew to a close. Things had not been the same since her breakdown. Depression and fear, like the little demons they are, continued to dominate her emotionally. She had some good days, however, and was quite productive when her "sun was shining." She took it on herself and arranged for Jim to have an office space in the basement of a dormitory; she raised the money, purchased the furniture, and did the decorating in what she described as "Early Flea Market" style. All this had been a surprise for Jim and he was deeply appreciative, but this kind of support from Maxine was increasingly rare.

In post seminary days we see a woman in conflict, as in this photo. On the back Maxine wrote "Sharp Jim and missionary Maxine." She'd come a long way from her pageant pictures of a few years earlier. Religion kills and destroys.

Max was hard to figure. On this day her sun was shining. She is still a rather striking lady here. But Jim only saw her like this a few days per month. Increasingly, her sun was failing to rise.

Fueling her problems with depression, Max had been suffering severe lower back pain since the latter half of 1938. It was diagnosed as a compressed lumbar disc, the result of an earlier automobile accident. Max was deteriorating. She no long felt good physically or emotionally. The "Christian" religion she'd acquired was not helping. The harder she tried to emulate the accepted "Christian" norms in dress, appearance, vocabulary, and life-style, the worse she became. She could not save her soul by burying her spirit. Prior to her back problems, for example, Max had loved to dance. But as dancing was considered sinful, she had given it up.

Jim and Maxine had much to learn about communication, for neither was able to understand what was happening to the other. Ironically, the man that God was using to reach young people with the life-giving message of Christ seldom conversed with his wife about the subject. One night he wrote in his journal:

> *It is a real rebuke to my own heart that I have not often talked to Maxine of the Lord's precious dealings in my own life. May the Lord become daily more precious to her in a life of complete yieldedness to his perfect will.*

Jim gave himself, heart and soul, to the development of the Miracle Book Clubs, but his work with kids was done in his own way and in his own style. It was certainly not his style to take his marching orders from elderly church women. Increasingly, some of Jim's work with kids was done under a different banner. Sometimes the kids who were involved in Jim's M.B.C. chapters were recruited to help sponsor and promote his other projects, done under this new name. It was all ministry to Jim, and for a period in 1940 and early 1941, his work was also done under the name of the 'Young Life Campaign,' a name he said he 'stole' from a group in England.

Maxine: "If the truth be told, very few people in Texas had ever heard of the Miracle Book Club. It was not a work that was having a big impact on Texas teenagers, nor a work that was likely to attract Jim, who got involved simply because he liked the name. But suddenly the Miracle Book Club had something to talk about; Jim's results with the Gainesville kids were simply unheard of."

On Thursday, May 9th, 1940, the Gainesville Daily Register reported that Jim had been appointed to a full time position as state director of the Miracle Book Club, resigning his position as director of young people's work at the First Presbyterian Church. Maxine recalled, "A newspaper article can give a pretty erroneous impression, as this one did. Since Jim's church position didn't pay, and the M.B.C. position didn't pay, this headline was more fluff than substance. With no income to speak of, there really wasn't a position to resign from, and in the same way, there wasn't much of a position to go to."

In the summer of 1940, following his graduation, Jim went all over south Texas setting up contacts for more high school clubs. Under the new name of "Young Life Campaign," he held tent meetings in Houston, Dallas, and Gainesville. These were evangelistic crusades complete with a choir, quartet, and preaching. There was even a children's meeting. Several of the kids involved in Jim's M.B.C. groups were asked to speak, sing, and assist in the new "Young Life" tent campaigns. Jim's journal records his progress in Dallas:

8/18: *We started Dallas YLC (Young Life Campaign) today— 220 in afternoon and 350 at evening meeting. I've not been at my best today—probably due to physical condition, but the Lord has greatly blessed.*

8/19: *51 at the children's meeting—260 tonight.*

8/20: *105 at children's meeting—325 in the evening. Excellent! The Lord seemed to especially bless.*

8/21: *Our smallest crowd of this campaign—about 200. Good interest however. 135 at children's meeting.*

8/22: *High school night—119 students—our biggest crowd to date—about 400 total. Really praise the Lord for today. Had wonderful time of prayer both before and after the meeting.*

8/27: *Big crowd tonight for high school night. 450 total, and 148 high school kids. Fine attention in spite of storm.*

That summer Jim spoke to thirteen-thousand people in his canvas tent. Approximately one-third were of high school age. From June through August, he led forty-two services in the tent, spoke four times over the radio, led eleven club meetings with the high school crowd, spoke at six church services in various cities, led two kids' camps, took twenty-one trips, had fifteen get-togethers with interested adults, spent seven days building tents, spoke at Rotary and Kiwanis three times, and saw Max through her second nervous breakdown.

Despite Maxine's pressing needs, Jim's life had become a feverish series of clubs to lead, sermons to preach, tents to build, classes to teach, and many other functions. He was excited about his budding vineyard, deeply touched by his sense of God's Spirit upon him, and convinced that in the high school crowd he had a responsive audience. Maxine, not having found the intimate relationship with Christ that Jim was experiencing, couldn't possibly understand his dedication.

As the 1940-41 school year began, the young couple had to vacate their apartment at school. On moving day, Jim spoke at the Dallas Seminary chapel. Dr. Chafer had asked him to present his work with the high school crowd. The next day Jim started teaching a class about Young Life. As a result of his chapel talk, sixty-five fellows signed up.

Little did the men in Jim's class know how quickly he would have them at the front lines. Many had come to his class to gain insights they could use later, but Jim was a recruiter, and his enthusiasm was contagious. Within days, many of these men found themselves walking around a high school campus in Houston, Dallas, or Gainesville, making friends with kids and promoting the new clubs.

As his work continued to prosper, Jim's situation at home continued to decline. His 1940 journal records his success at work and his problems at home:

10/10: *Left early for Houston. Had a good contact at Addicks High School. Fine rally tonight. Made plans for six new clubs to start Thursday, one week from today. Maxine bad tonight.*

10/14: *Many contacts today. Good meeting in Gainesville but only sixty-five. Coleman began at St. Joe with twenty kids. Harry had twenty at Myra. Maxine's condition bad.*

10/17: *An excellent time with John E. Mitchell this a.m. Took little Ann with me today. Maxine not well.*

10/18: *Around home after shopping with Maxine and Ann. Maxine really bad tonight.*

10/29: *Maxine very bad this a.m. so I called off everything and came home. Made an appointment with the doctor for tomorrow.*

10/30: *Took Maxine to the doctor (psychiatrist). He was frank to say there may be no easy or inexpensive way out for us.*

10/31: *I picked up a mob of roughnecks tonight out in Harrisburg—some of them said they would come to YL next week. God seemed to lead to these guys.*

11/1: *Maxine very bad.*

11/6: *Maxine's doctor is definite. She needs to go to hospital.*

11/7: *Excellent Houston trip. Little Ann went with me. Three of the guys I picked up last week came to club. They were interested, too. God is faithful.*

11/8: *Returned from Houston in a.m. Felt bum—severe migraine—relief with shot. Maxine bad.*

11/9: *Took Maxine to hospital this a.m. Hated to leave her out there. Left for Houston on 5:00 p.m. train.*

Ann was three years old, Mary Margaret eight months, when Max was hospitalized. When he could manage, Jim took Ann with him; when he couldn't, she stayed with friends in Gainesville. Mary Margaret (Sue) was cared for by Ted and Mary Lou Benson, one of the young couples at seminary who had joined Jim in developing his fledging work with high school kids.

Three weeks after entering the hospital, Max was released. Her condition was no different from before. Prior to her breakdown, few things had given Jim more pleasure than coming home to Max and his "cute girlies," but coming home was no longer joyful. As Jim recorded in his journal entry of December 8:

> A bad day. All family feeling bad and Maxine apparently doing no good. But we had a wonderful time of prayer together about it tonight. I believe the Lord, and He alone, can solve our problem.

In spite of increasing marital problems, Jim's efforts to reach high school kids continued to produce a healthy crop. Doors were opening on all sides. Supporters began pressuring him to incorporate his work, largely as a means of giving donors a tax deduction. Jim hadn't given this issue a great deal of thought. His heart was in presenting Jesus Christ to the high school crowd; if incorporating would benefit the cause, Jim would vote for it. On December 24, 1940, the Young Life Campaign board of directors was formed. The initial group was composed of Dr. Chafer, Ted Benson, John E. Mitchell, and Jim. Legal papers of incorporation were filed ten months later.

Jim was later to feel that he was caught napping on this issue. At first, the idea seemed heaven-sent, as he had three dedicated and gifted men with him to chart the course ahead and help steer the ship. Jim failed to consider, however, the long-range ramifications of incorporating. One of several questions is whether the Christ teaching can successfully be married to the "corporate way," as a "Christian organization" is an oxymoron of sorts (but that's another book). Secondly, Jim had, without thinking, given people down the road the authority to dismiss him from his life's work should they no longer support him. He could regret that deeply, given the right circumstances.

Early in 1941, Jim decided to have a mass Young Life rally in downtown Dallas at the Baker Hotel. Several of the men assisting him were dubious about the plan, but as usual, Jim's opinion prevailed. "This is the Red Letter Day!" Jim wrote in red, in his journal of February 24, 1941. "Attendance at the Young Life mass meeting at the Baker Hotel was 2,000, and many were crowded out. Program superb—great spirit—especially among the men of the school."

On the very next day, in stark contrast to this elation, Jim's journal references his deteriorating relationship with Mrs. McClusky and her Bible Club hostesses:

> All day with Mrs. McClusky. Very uncomfortable deal trying to get out from under the load of this M.B.C. mess.

The next day Jim writes:

> Migraine tonight. Really a terrible experience this evening trying to get the (M.B.C.) hostesses to see the necessity for my leaving M.B.C. Never got in such a hard place. Don't believe we are getting to first base with these women.

On March 19, Jim enters:

> A great day. "Young Life Clubs" came into being—unanimously voted by 23 fellows of the teaching force—the name—the motto (Christ is Life)—the verse (I John 5:12).

> 3/22/1941: A very full day climaxed by a mess of a meeting with the hostesses (M.B.C.) that just left me worn out and sick. There is NO USE ever trying to get along with that outfit. Praise the Lord for at least keeping us sweet!

Two days later Jim changed the name of his Gainesville Miracle Book Club to the Gainesville Young Life Club, and he never looked back. The kids really didn't care what the name was, they were there because of Jim, and they enthusiastically voted for the name change.

Hardly a day went by that Jim wasn't speaking on the radio, in a church, to a Rotary meeting, in a high school, a Masonic Home, or in another city. And the more he spoke, the faster the invitations rolled in. At times he was speaking to six or more different groups all in one day. It was all he could do to keep up with the demands of his hectic schedule. In one thirty-four-day stretch in 1941, during a trip to the Midwest and East Coast, he spoke seventy-nine times.

Back in Texas, things continued to boom, as his 1942 journal describes:

2/7: One of the busiest days I ever had. Mailed out 850 letters to mailing list, and 50 personal letters to various leaders. Really do not know how to tackle this stupendous job. Exhausted.

2/9: A great day in Tyler with fifty kids in a fair meeting tonight. A particularly fine group of kids. Add and Loveta drove me to the railroad and I went to bed.

2/10: Club #37 was the best we have ever had and perhaps about the best club meeting I was ever in. The Holy Spirit was manifestly present, and the whole program went over well with the young people. One fellow accepted the Lord.

This entry is of particular interest as it is the first time Jim referred to his and Orville Mitchell's club as Club #37. There weren't thirty-six others, of course, but if Jim was talking to kids in Houston about starting a club in their school, this allowed him to say, "Why, in Dallas at Club #37 last week we had one-hundred kids show up." The kids Jim was talking to would naturally assume there were thirty-six other clubs that had preceded #37. They figured, "Wow, this must really be a going concern. When can we get a club started?" Jim had never said there were thirty-six others, he just named that one #37. Jim's 1942 journal continues:

2/18: My best work at Masonic Home when I gave both clubs the Gospel very straight from (Girls) John 2 and (Boys) John 6:1 and following. An amazing response to invitation to openly confess Christ: those who have received Him since the meetings began—20 girls, 15 fellows.

2/23: Fifteen-hundred at the Roof garden Rally. The crowd not as big as last year, but the program was snappier and went over with a great "bang."

2/24: A marvelous crowd of nearly a thousand, practically filling the huge Rice Ball Room (Houston).

2/27: The San Antonio mass meeting was "beyond that which we ask or think"—a great time. Everyone very happy about the whole thing. I took 11:00 P.M. train for home.

3/1: The closing service (in Waco) of the Mass Meeting Week was a great thrill. The Lord greatly blessed and the after-meeting was wonderful. A large number of Baylor students really touched! Praise the Lord for His wonderful working this week.

3/3: A great meeting of #37 tonight. Figured the financial needs for the budget and mass meeting today and am $250.00 short. Maxine and I committed it to Lord.

3/4: Another of those red letter days! A check from Orville Mitchell, postmarked yesterday 3 p.m.—amount $250.00. Just wipes out our deficit. It is AMAZING to see how the Lord works. Then tonight. How He did work at the Masonic Home where 12 more girls accepted the Lord as Savior.

3/7: A very profitable and busy day at the office. Nice evening at home with the girlies! They are so sweet!

Jim was a hard-driving man, frequently working to the point of exhaustion. His fledgling work with kids had hardly left the cradle stage before the demands of fund raising, mailing lists, newsletters, recruiting, training, teaching, and travel almost overwhelmed him. Maxine recalls: "It just killed me to see Jim push himself so hard. I figured I was going to lose him early, as I couldn't see how a person could drive himself like that and not have it catch up with him sooner or later. When I brought the subject up, Jim always said he would rather burn out than rust out. Personally, I never understood why someone should have to do either.

"He definitely believed his steps were ordered of the Lord. Believing this with all his heart, he trusted that he wouldn't take a wrong step, that the Lord would keep him on the road he should travel. I wished, however, that I could wave a little magic wand and say, 'Relax, Relax.' I always wanted him to take it easier, to spend more time with his family. It hurt me to see him in a tied-up condition."

Jim lived his life at a rapid pace, but he did something few Christians do—he bathed his every move in prayer. These excerpts from his 1941-1944 journals show the importance of prayer to his work, and the place of humility in his heart:

Enroute (on train) and evening in New Orleans. A truly remarkable day. The lord wonderfully enabled me to spend almost the entire day in prayer. Didn't eat lunch but continued on in prayer as He led and it was a blessed time.

I gave a Gospel message and 8 young people of high school age accepted Christ as their Savior! Three splendid fellows made complete surrender of their lives to Him. WONDERFUL a.m. service. [Spoke on "PEACE"] Not the liberty I wanted but HE blessed. The people fell on my neck. How can I ever measure up to these dear people's expectations of me.

I felt most happy about the day and have much warm gratitude to God for all that He has done. It must be ALL of Him. I certainly have nothing to offer.

Had the best time of prayer of my whole life tonight. Did not feel like praying but knew I needed to more than anything. Just took the Lord at his Word and went to him with everything. He gave me great peace. As I study this thing, I am convinced that times of unrest are always due to failure in prayer.

Busy day at office—then to train. Little Ann going with me. She went right to sleep as soon as we climbed in our upper berth. Was so weary I couldn't pray very well. Oh, that I might never have days too busy to pray.

Had very precious times of prayer today. Oh that God will just draw out this sorry heart of mine in real burden of prayer.

It would be impossible to really describe this day. My heart completely overflows with gratitude and praise to God for His Faithfulness in the face of my own unbelief and for what HE has wrought in the hearts of these dear young people. Surely well over 100 testimonies without the least bit of persuasion. Many young people (perhaps 15 or 20) really professed openly faith in Christ as Savior for the first time. Great spirit among leaders and young people as well. The HOLY SPIRIT is here in power! Feel better than for months spiritually, physically and all. II Timothy 2:13.

I have been getting a great blessing out of "Bush Aglow." I pray that the Lord will start The Fire in me.

Received great blessing from finishing "Bush Aglow." It's greatest punch is supplied by the marvelous evidence that God will USE what is turned over to Him. If we WANT to be used HE is willing—it is just "our human best"—all of it that HE wants. Filled with His Holy Spirit it is ENOUGH!

Greatly enjoyed "Borden of Yale" today. Believe that God would still bring to pass such things as his and Moody's experience if we would but let him. How I long to get "hands off" completely of my own affairs and let Him reign supreme on the Throne of my life.

Spoke to total of 1300 young people this week! Good Saturday night crowd in spite of afternoon rain and very wet ground. My sermon on "The Love of God" was quite FLAT I feel. But the Lord seemed very definitely to bless.

I am miserable. Filled with unrest and nervous and do not feel close to the Lord.

Rose at 4:50 this a.m. and spent from then till 6:00 a.m. in prayer. Oh how I long to go on with HIM 100%, gaining strength, grace, and wisdom for whatever each day may bring—in the stillness of His Presence before the day begins. Only by His en-

abling grace will I ever do it! In myself I am the world's biggest flop.

Young people seem to be going rapidly nowhere for the Lord. (That is probably because I am not really ministering in the fullness of the Spirit myself lately). Oh that I could just LET God work out His life in me. Problems seem to drive me away from the Lord instead of toward him.

Had a grand hike up the Oak Creek Trail (in Colorado) today. Enjoyed it immensely and had a wonderful time of prayer up on the mountain on the return trip.

A wonderful half-hour of prayer this a.m. I have been convicted more and more about the many days that I do not really have much time ALONE for prayer—so I have asked the Lord to get me up early and let me experience Psalm 143:8 (Let the morning bring me word of your unfailing love for I have put my trust in you. Show me the way I should go, for to you I lift up my soul." New International Version}. He answered and gave me a real touch this a.m.

He got me up—in answer to definite prayer and I had the most down to business time of prayer that I have had for a long time. Now for the new year, my main objective is that 1943 shall be a "prayer year"—much more than ever before.

5:30 A.M. This has been the finest start I have ever made in a new year. Went to bed at 11:30 with a miserable headache. With no effort on my part, simply committing it to Him, He woke me at 4:00 a.m. without any headache and gave me the sweetest time of fellowship with Himself that I have ever had— at least for a long time. My heart was open to confess my sin and failure and there was plenty of it. By His grace I knew that I really hated that sin and longed to be cleansed of it—and He kept His promise (I John 1:9). The Lord led me to really commit the year 1943 to Him and I prayed especially that my life might be more of a testimony to my own dear wife and kiddies and the ones who work with me. More definitely than ever I have committed the coming days, projects, growth, plans to Him. Now to LET GO and LET GOD.

Chicago—One of the grandest and MOST DEFINITE answers to prayer I have ever had. Just before leaving the room at 7:15 I prayed that the Lord would let me go home tonight. Had I gone without praying I would have missed the phone call telling me of a seat on 9:00 Braniff to Dallas. PRAISE HIM. Deuteronomy 32:4.

Word—one hour, Prayer—one and a half hours. I have been getting about the greatest blessing of my whole life recently from a study of Pierson's "Life of George Mueller." It has HIT ME HARD and THE LORD has brought deep conviction about my own awful sin of prayerlessness and lack of Faith—(my) lack of zeal and earnestness in prayer. By His grace I am asking for a real turning point in my life. It is time to turn up the path of "Dead to Jim Rayburn"—his desires, comforts, etc. and (begin) seeking to win no acclaim or approval but God's.

Wrote letters, studied, and prayed this a.m. after sleeping late. Spoke this evening on "Life's Greatest Opportunity," using Luke 18:35-42. Small crowd but much good accomplished by the Holy Spirit, I believe. I have a deep and abiding feeling of His presence, a sense of real yieldedness to Him, dating from a special experience of surrender and dedication to the Eternal Light, which I experienced Saturday night in my room.

I pray for a sufficient measure of His grace to do what is pleasing to Him in the office and in all dealings with the staff. Oh, Father, make us READY and WILLING to have no other purpose than to exalt Christ.

1 hour in the Word, 4 hours and 15 minutes prayer. No doubt this is the greatest New Year's experience ever and one of the greatest experiences of my life. After Maxine went to bed Add and I continued on in the most wonderful season of prayer

*until 4 a.m. Also great fellowship and sense of communion with
the Lord. We really turned things over to Him. There is great
conviction of Sin re. Matthew 7:7. The awful fact that many
things we need from God we do not ASK FOR and do not stay
with Him when we do. DEEP Conviction also concerning
Prayerlessness and Failure to Study the Word, and (our failure
to) love Prayer and Word. By HIS grace—not this year.*

*Word—40 min., Prayer—4 hr., 30 min., 10 min., 29 min.
Beyond doubt I am experiencing the most wonderful season of
my Christian Life with respect to the FIRST thing: my personal
relationship with the Lord. This day, from 12:30 a.m. until 5:00
a.m. was perhaps the most wonderful season of prayer I have
ever had. And completely "beyond me". Almost the entire time
on my knees—without migraines and a real sense of the Spirit of
prayer. All thru the night Matthew 7:7, John 16:24, Romans
8:26-27, Hebrews 4:16 were very precious and the Lord just
thrilled my heart all day with Psalms 16:11. Oh to let Him show
me this every step of the way. A wonderful time of prayer with
the girls this a.m. Real burden for the school. And the Lord is
blessing the work so much—just in the matter of John 13:34, 35
especially. Got stuck in the mud on Concho St!*

All day in prayer—no doubt the greatest day I've ever had.

It was this daily, prayerful dedication of his life, energy, and
talents that opened many doors. In his efforts to meet and befriend
America's high school kids, Jim had no proven method on which he
could rely. Sometimes he would hang around a high school until
someone asked him, "What do you do, Jim?" And he'd say, "I lead
Young Life Clubs."

"Young Life Clubs?"

"Yeah. Haven't you ever heard of Young Life Clubs?"

"Well, no . . ."

"You've never heard of Young Life? Why, it's the greatest thing
happening! Last week in Dallas, at Club #37, we had a hundred kids
show up. In Tyler High School, over fifty kids come to Young Life

every week! And you thought you knew what was going on around here, didn't you?"

Of course they'd never heard of it. There weren't any clubs in their town. So he'd lead them on, "It's the greatest thing! You don't know about it? Tell you what . . . get your girls and meet me at the hotel Tuesday night. We'll have supper together and I'll tell you about it." Usually they showed up. The appeal was a winner with kids.

In the early forties Jim received several invitations to address a high school assembly. One appearance led to another, and these invitations poured in for nearly twenty years. In numerous high schools where Jim spoke, his was voted by the students to be the year's number one student assembly.

He really wowed the kids. He'd tell jokes for the first half of his talk—corny as can be, "High school isn't so bad, it's just the 'principle' of the thing." Kids would cheer and whoop and howl and the principal would get a little uneasy. Then he'd go on about "that cross-eyed teacher they had to fire because she couldn't see eye-to-eye with the principal." And, "I was talking to the principal this morning and he told me he just had to do something about all this kissing going on right under his nose."

The kids went wild! They didn't know who Jim was, but they knew he was funny, and they liked him. Then he'd tell them he was surprised that most people are so ignorant about the greatest story every told. "Since you kids want to be intelligent, and want your lives to work right, you at least ought to check out what I'm talking about." He challenged them; he dared them. "Don't be ignorant, don't turn thumbs down on the greatest proposition in the world until you've checked it out." Then he'd invite them to that evening's club. Within days, many of the kids were actively involved in Jim's meetings.

In city after city, Jim's new club was catching on. The staff was small, and it was not uncommon for a staff man to lead five clubs in five different cities. People pushed themselves to keep pace with Jim. After a particularly heavy week of assemblies, Jim was heard to say, "One of the reasons I'm eager for heaven is to see if these things do any good. Why, I'm so tired, the seat of my pants is wiping out my footprints."

Young Life's original staff of five men, led by Jim, had moved west, south, and east from Gainesville and Dallas. The salary was one hundred dollars per month. There was about the whole venture a simplicity and directness. There were no benefits or future guarantees, just the present moment to be spent in Christ's service.

Quoting Jim, "I graduated from Dallas Seminary with a wife, two baby girls, a five-dollar bill, and a wonderful sense of the Lord's leading—that the Lord wanted me to stay with those kids and He'd take care of the rest. I had the great joy and privilege of finding out like I never could have discovered had I gone into a salaried position, that the Lord certainly does take care and keep his promises. That five dollar bill was soon spent and we didn't have anything.

"Our daughter Sue was on a Carnation milk formula, and one night at dinner Maxine said, 'Well, Jim, our little girl has just enough formula for her ten p.m. feeding, then we're out.' I said, 'That so? We'd better pray about that hadn't we?' Max was half way down on her knees before I said that. So we prayed, and then I took off to a meeting with a committee of folks who wanted to assist me in the Dallas work. Funniest committee you ever saw! There were five or six people and one was a girl who worked in the slums. She was paid eight dollars a month, and paid her mother five dollars per month for room and board. She was really loaded you can see. All those people were poverty stricken folks. So we had this meeting and she came up to me afterward and handed me a little brown paper sack. She said the girls she worked with (all homeless destitute people) had heard about what Maxine and I were going to do and had taken their savings and wanted to give it to us as an offering. I took that sack and nearly ran across the seminary campus where we were still living. Max and I opened up that sack and laid out the money and it was eighty-six cents, from the poorest people in the world. I went out to one of those late ice houses in Dallas and bought eighty-six cents worth of Carnation milk. We just went on feeding the formula and trusting the Lord. We were scared to death a lot of the time. We used to actually resent it when people would say we'd gone out on faith, because we knew we didn't have any faith. We were scared and we wondered whether we'd done the right thing and we'd do all this figuring and wondering. We just went out on the Lord's faithfulness, that's all. This business of going out on faith, that's kind of malarkey. We don't have much faith, any of us. But God is so faithful that He'll take care of anyone who is set on going His way."

Jim had placed his families' needs and the needs of his staff in God's care. His May 1, 1941 journal:

> *Today marks the beginning of our second year of just look-ing to the Lord to provide our material needs. It is amazing to find that in the first year of 'no salary' living our income has been (coded numerals). I can't believe it—in view of my own failures in prayer and service. It is ALL our blessed Lord!*

Max and Jim's sweet 'girlies,' Ann and Sue, Mesa Verde, 1942

Jim had entered into the fire of testing and purification; little did he know how those flames would soon be fanned. Attempts to destroy and discredit him were lurking round the bend.

Big Ideas

BLISTERING charges of undermining church youth work were hurled at Jim from several of the major denominations. A Dallas association of religious educators and ministers from some twenty-five Protestant churches published specific criticisms. Front-page headlines in one church publication condemned him as a "shameful sham." The story quoted church leaders, saying that Young Life was "irreverent . . . definitely harmful to the minds of young people."

Criticism mounted from all sides. "Jim Rayburn is taking kids away from church. The music sung at Young Life clubs is jazz. Emotionalism runs high. Young Life is communist, a cult, politically subversive. Sensationalism reigns supreme." In short, Jim was found guilty without a trial. These attacks upon Jim and his Young Life work by the mainline denominations were to be a constant trial and tribulation for the next quarter-century. Jim was a church boy himself, his father an evangelist; it felt as if his own family had stabbed him in the back.

Jim had never given a thought to fighting the church, or to taking kids away from it. He was simply burdened that so many teens ignorantly turn their backs on the greatest offer ever made to them. He wanted to present the life, love, and glorious news of what Jesus Christ had done for man in the warmest, most exciting way possible. A majority of churches had quit being warm and exciting long before Jim came on the scene. Further, the kids Jim was attempting to reach were not church kids. But trouble began when the church kids discovered Jim. He was a breath of fresh air to most of them; some, preferring Jim's meeting to their weekly youth group, dropped out of church. A few of those who met Jim recall their impressions:

"I went to a camp for kids, and there I met the man who was to become the greatest single influence on my life, Jim Rayburn. He shared his life, gave to me of himself, and influenced me in a way no other human being has ever done."

"The greatest man I ever met—my life has not been the same from the day he first spoke to me. I may have never discovered that I could know God in a personal way had I not met him."

"A visionary, and a man with the faith to see those visions through."

"There was something burning in him—you could see it in his eyes."

What was burning in Jim's eyes is that which burns in the eyes of all men and women who know the wonder of God's indwelling Spirit. To be indwelled by the Sprit of God is the doorway into the fourth dimension, the realm of spirit, and the kingdom of God. It is an awesome, joyful, liberating experience that has no adequate earthly explanation. When the marvelous revelation of God's reality and goodness is experienced by a mortal, he will agonize to share that experience with those he loves. To hold the "living water" in your hand and see your brother dying of thirst because he refuses to drink, is to share in heavenly sorrow. Christ wept over it, and those who really know him do the same.

Jim was not an organizer, but an agonizer, frequently spending more time in prayer than in his office. He felt that the twentieth-century "Christian" church had a woeful shortage of agonizers. "Christian organizations," as well, are loaded to the brim with organizers: time-management specialists, fund raisers, public relations experts, business experts, camping industry experts, administrative experts, every kind of expert, but sometimes few, or maybe none, of God's anointed. Jim had no desire to start another such organization. "I always feel a tinge of embarrassment," he'd later say in that slow drawl, "when I'm introduced as the founder of this outfit" (Young Life), "cause I never had any idea I was founding anything. I am the founder, don't get me wrong, but it seems to me that the founder of something ought to at least know he was founding something, and I never did."

By the mid forties, Jim was speaking at 150 high school assemblies per year and leading three to four Young Life clubs. He traveled extensively to promote the work, see his staff, and run a summer camping program for high school kids.

On October 31, 1945, Maxine gave birth to their third and last child, James C. Rayburn III (the author of this book). Jim recorded in his journal:

> Maxine and my little son came home today. He is very cute, and sweet, and I am a very proud pop. I just can't believe what is happening at Riverside High School . . . .

Jim became a father figure to a far wider group than his immediate family. He filled that role for some of his staff and no doubt hundreds of high school kids as well. He divided his schedule as best he knew, but there wasn't enough time or energy to cover all the bases. With Maxine's health and emotions on the ebb, Jim tried his best to fill in the void. He tenderly wrote in his 1944 journal:

> 10/20: Worked hard at office and then took Ann (age 7) to her school dinner and carnival tonight. It was a mob, but I so enjoy doing things with the kiddies.

> 10/21: Took the kids to the circus this afternoon. Enjoyed it greatly, but I am very weary. Have been extremely worn out lately, to the point of exhaustion. Fun to be with the "girlies."

By 1946, the Young Life staff had grown to twenty men and women; they could be found in Tyler, Houston, Dallas, Memphis, Tulsa, Chicago, Seattle, Portland, Bellingham, Yakima, and Mexico. All were attempting to look to God. Yet, most looked to Jim for their encouragement, help, training, and finances.

If there's a good excuse for exhaustion, Jim had it. The demands of Young Life were pushing him to his limit, his wife's health was a constant concern, and he fought an endless war with his own health problems. From 1940 through 1946, he had two major surgical procedures performed on his abdomen, a yearly operation on his nose, and an ongoing battle with intense migraine headaches which sapped him of strength. Migraines had been a curse for Jim since the age of four. Intense pain that peaked gradually was often accompanied by nausea. Jim was neither a hypochondriac nor a complainer; he truly suffered with this problem. From the onset of the symptoms through the termination of the headache, he was usually laid up for forty-eight hours. Rarely do his diaries fail to record the number of days since the last migraine. Each headache might cost him two days of productivity, and he could usually count on three a month. It was a lifelong plague.

The strain of Maxine's deteriorating health added to the stress Jim endured. He simply had no place to escape life's pressures and problems. The more he sought refuge in his work, the worse the problems became at home. "Since age fourteen," Maxine recalled, "I was very sensitive about being rejected. I understood Jim's usual absence as a reflection of me—as if I had been abandoned again or wasn't wanted. I hadn't found Christ, peace, love, or joy in Christianity—I had no personal knowledge of the Holy Spirit—so I really didn't understand what was happening spiritually to Jim. At times I made things pretty rough on him. Not knowing the power available to me, I fought life's problems in my own strength—and lost."

Maxine's lower back problem worsened each time she gave birth. After my birth, it was necessary to hire help, as she could no longer bend, lift, or carry. Living with intense pain only weakened her emotions further.

Tired, burdened, and lonely, in the midst of a vicious attack by the church, his marriage suffering, the demands of his work pushing him to his limit, Jim's undying faith and God-given love for kids drove him on. While on a trip to Colorado Springs, October 16, 1944, he spoke to thirty-nine-hundred kids in one day. That night he wrote in his journal:

What a day! Five assemblies! Every one of them just rolled. I can never thank the Lord enough for HIS grace and power to make us acceptable to all these kids.

I cannot write of tonight. Surely I have never been privileged to see anything like it. In one day's time—this great throng of young people. And the presence and power of the Lord by the Holy Spirit every moment of the way.

By his Grace alone I was enabled to produce the best day's ministry of my life. Tonight I gave the most forceful Gospel message I have ever given. The response of these dear and precious kids was like nothing I have ever seen before. All the boys agree that this was our greatest day in Young Life work. I know God hears and answers prayer.

10/17: I began this day just after midnight seeking the Lord's face in grateful PRAISE for yesterday, and with all my heart dedicating myself anew to the proposition of being absolutely all out for Him, all the time.

If truth be told, most Christians really struggle with prayer. At the root of this conflict is that age old demon, unbelief. We don't really believe, bottom line, that prayer will make a difference, or that God will really listen and respond. Jim knew better:

11/8: This has been one of the truly great days of my life. Shortly after going to bed last night, about 1:00 a.m., I became very restless. Soon got up, read the Word, and prayed. The Lord met me in such a strange and warm way as I bared my heart before him until nearly 5:00 a.m. Then up at 6:30 and out to pray with the men. Came right back here where I spent the whole morning and much of the afternoon in prayer and study of the Victorious Life. Oh, the joy of realizing that He is right here!

11/9: Another unbelievably wonderful day. The Lord is doing something to me that has never happened before—giving me such a desire to be absolutely sold out to Jesus Christ and completely dead to self and all else that the world holds. I spent almost all day in prayer yesterday and today. It seems that my heart is almost to break just to completely enter into the truth of ALL THINGS IN JESUS I FIND.

Now it is 1:30 a.m. I have lost much sleep this week and have not experienced THE LEAST BIT of weariness in my work. The Lord Jesus is more precious to me than ever before . I want to know what it means to SUFFER FOR JESUS' SAKE. May the Lord Jesus, by his Spirit, deal with me until truly CHRIST BE FORMED IN ME (Gal 4:19).

12/18: Prayer this a.m. Then off for a busy day. At nearly midnight had a time alone with the Lord in prayer. He met me in a way that has seldom, if ever, happened before. Was the greatest time of worship I can remember. How sure I was that I could not in the least be fooling Jesus, or pretending to surrender. Had perfect liberty to acknowledge that I was offering myself completely to Him, regardless—Col. 4:12. Was flooded with unspeakable peace. God was with me in a more intimate way than I have ever known before. My greatest desire was to worship and thank him, though much of the time I could not express any thought in words at all. I hope and pray that memory will serve me to recall whatever of this precious time alone with God I need to remember for His Glory in days ahead. Am quite sure I have never gone through such a season of testing, and have been "shown up" as never before as to my "utter unreliability"—so this Mercy and Sovereign Grace of my God means more to me than ever before. I DO NOT WANT ANYTHING IN MY LIFE THAT IS NOT OF THE LORD JESUS.

The faith of those who know this intimacy with Christ is seldom understood by others. In Jim's case, almost every idea the Spirit laid on his heart was contested by those around him. Such was the case when Jim first felt the need to purchase a summer resort for kids. By 1945, he was actively looking for a campsite in Colorado. As salaries were minimal for Young Life staff, few could understand his conviction. Some thought he was crazy. Where would the money come from? Jim didn't have the answer, but he trusted God to provide.

In the spring of 1946, Herb Taylor, president of the Young Life board of directors, received a call from Jim regarding a property known as Star Ranch, a beautiful facility just five miles south of Colorado Springs. Together with his wife, Gloria, Mr. Taylor flew to Colorado, looked over the ranch, and gave a thousand-dollar check as earnest money.

A board of directors meeting was hastily arranged to discuss the purchase. Several expressed a fear that Jim wanted the property for his own personal enjoyment. Some felt that kids from other parts of the country would have no interest in Colorado. Most were afraid to take on such a financial burden. Incredible as it seems many years later, there was not one vote besides Herb's and Jim's to continue with the purchase. Although Jim had dynamic and unusual leadership abilities, and covered every step he took with hours of prayer, he was constantly questioned by his associates, both on his board of directors as well as his staff. Herb Taylor, fortunately, had the vision necessary to recognize the Lord's hand on Jim's life.

Herb, as a staunch believer in Jim's vision, left the meeting, sold part of his stock in Club Aluminum, and purchased Star Ranch himself. He leased the property to Young Life for one dollar per year; later, he donated it.

That some believed Jim's interest in a camping property was simply selfish shows how little these men understood what was happening in their midst. They were in the company of a young David, and few felt he should tackle Goliath-size projects.

In future years Jim would be drained of much energy by persistent struggles with a doubting staff and board of directors. Jim trusted the inner prompting of the Spirit, but seemed destined to carry a doubting group of associates on his shoulders.

Jim had one very close friend, a man who understood him and whose faith was his inspiration—Sid Smith, from Winnipeg, Canada. In spiritual matters, Sid was Jim's big brother. He understood the consuming fire within Jim as no others did, and his company was a treat Jim savored, as these journal entries of 1947 testify:

1/28: *A wonderful day in Winnipeg. Assemblies at Kelvin and St. James Collegiate were too good to be true. Five radio broadcasts. Young Life quartet was good, Orien Johnson excellent. Twenty below zero, but a larger crowd than last night. Great to be with Sid. He's great!*

1/29: *Don't see how the Lord can bless me so much in this work that's so dear to my heart. Very large crowd tonight. Good meeting at Rotary for lunch, very well received. Sid and I had one of those sweet, intimate times of fellowship such as I never had with anyone but him. Thank God for it all!*

Days with Sid Smith—what special days they were for Jim. What a joy to have a brother with real faith, a brother who understood him. This friendship was truly a gift to a man who was lonely in his faith, and what a shock it was when Sid died, two days later:

1/31: Sid went home today. It was quick and quiet at 5:00 p.m. He was taken away to meet the Savior he loved. Of all the sweet memories I shall carry through life of this dearest friend God ever gave me—this is paramount. SID LOVED JESUS! Like John of old he loved Him because HE KNEW HIM. Sid taught me of Jesus and his great love as no other man ever did. He taught me what friendship means. He was my friend and I shall never forget him. He loved me—my heart rejoices in that. I wonder why it was so?

Sid often told me so sincerely, "Jim, no matter what you ever did I would love you. No matter what you say, I will stand by you." He meant it! What a guy! His last week on earth was the happiest week of my life. God's wonderful Grace shining through Sid Smith made it so. I want to love Jesus like Sid did. He loved the Savior so much that he even loved LITTLE GUYS too. Like Jesus did! We carried on at the chapel tonight for God and for Sid. It was lonely up there. The Lord gave us a wonderful meeting with more young people accepting Christ than any other time. Wonderful time at Gordon Bell this morning. A grand luncheon at H. Gary. Sid was there, happy and pulling for me as always.

Years later, Sid's family would donate their summer residence to Jim's Young Life work. Thousands of America's teenagers would spend the best week of their lives at the Castaway Club in Detroit Lakes, Minnesota. This beautiful facility is a unique memorial to the special love and friendship shared by these two dearest of friends.

Shortly after Sid's death, Jim and Max uprooted their three young Texans and moved to Star Ranch, joining Charlie and Harriet Johnson, who had already settled in with their three young children. Jim commuted between Dallas and Colorado Springs for several months. Then, the entire headquarters was moved into a log cabin in the woods. Jim's adversary was close behind.

Two Ranches

MOST American teenagers consider Christians dull. Multitudes of adults share this viewpoint that sees Christ as for old people, religious people, boring people, sick people, hypocritical people, or dead people. This tragic misconception, this ultimate lie, burdened Jim's heart. He had accepted the biblical perspective that Christ *is life.*, and that without an intimate relationship with God's indwelling spirit, a person is dead (Matt. 8:22).

Jim's resorts for kids gave him an opportunity to break down many misconceptions that kid's might hold regarding Christians, or Christianity. A week with Jim and his funny, talented followers was akin to a week on Fantasy Island. He did everything with a verve and zest that showed his love of life, and he seasoned it all with laughter. It was contagious, this constant urge to stretch every nerve and muscle, to laugh and laugh till your insides ached, and to go beyond the mundane patterns of life.

Although few had shared his vision of a camp in the Rocky Mountains, all were ecstatic when it materialized. Jim's staff bought bunk beds from a nearby military base, repaired and painted old furniture left at the ranch, and cleared ground for a baseball diamond and volleyball court. Everyone felt the spirit of excitement. A staff member recalls: "It was so beautiful we'd sleep outside in the summer. We were so excited we'd get up at four o'clock in the morning. We found some old horse blankets and I remember washing those by hand. You see, the ranch was ours, and we felt it. It was part and parcel of us. Our blood was in it."

The key to running a successful camp was quality. In a time when lean-tos, tent houses, and meager surroundings were synonymous with Christian camps, Jim insisted on excellence. He'd say, "Who started the idea that Christians ought to have the seat of their pants in patches, or that we ought to hold camps in tents? We talk about the King of Kings; let's act like He's the one in charge! We're gonna get the classiest camps in the country."

Jim had made a club leader of Orv Mitchell, a prominent Dallas businessman and member of Jim's board of directors for many years. Orv was the first to accompany a trainload of Texas kids to a Christmas camp where Jim was to speak. As they pulled into the train station at 5:30 in the morning, the Young Life brass band greeted them with a blasting reception; then a caravan of cars, overflowing with noisy, excited kids, wound south toward Star Ranch. At the darkest part of the road the caravan was stopped by a tall masked bandit (John Miller) who threatened to relieve everyone of their spending money. Orv's son Bob was driving the first car, and much to the horror of the kids, Bob took a very large pistol out of the glove compartment. With one left-handed shot, he dropped the bandit into a ditch and drove off. Within minutes of their arrival, the kids had received a noisy, enthusiastic welcome, been held up, and seen a gun fight. And they hadn't even reached the front gate; it wasn't yet time for breakfast!

After several days of high adventures, many laughs, great food, and thoughtful consideration of Jim's messages, the kids headed home. Some left with a new song in their heart, but everyone left knowing they'd experienced something special. That brief exposure to a gracious host and a loving atmosphere melted many false impressions of Christ.

Star Ranch did more than provide a resort for high school kids; it served as a center for bringing people together. Jim enjoyed having a showplace where he could welcome adults and share his vision. Numerous Colorado Springs couples caught that vision, gave generously of their time and money, and were instrumental in giving Jim's young work a foothold in Colorado.

Moving to the ranch provided Jim more time with Maxine and his children, extended exposure to the high school kids, and a quiet forest in which to listen for his Father's voice. But by 1947 Maxine's back problem had become acute, and the situation was affecting the whole family. On February 21, 1948, corrective surgery was attempted. Jim wrote:

> Maxine in surgery this a.m. She has extreme post-operative pain, but they are keeping her well sedated and she sleeps most of the time. Thank the Lord it is over with. Believe it will do the job.

Jim was flooded with relief; for the first time in years there was light at the end of the tunnel. It appeared the long, strenuous ordeal was over; there were better days ahead. But coming weeks would prove that the attempt to fuse bone chips into the herniated spinal disk had failed. Maxine's back pain was more intense than prior to surgery.

This operation's failure launched the family into an era of darkness. We were standing on the precipice of a bad dream. Maxine later recalled, "I was naive about drugs; it had never occurred to me to ask for a painkiller. But after the surgery I was given a large supply of Seconal to help me sleep. Soon I was reaching for a pill every time I felt pain, or discouragement. Before long, I was hooked. I had no idea of the devastation this would cause my family. By the time I recognized my dependence on these drugs, it was too late to stop. I felt I couldn't face life without them."

Maxine's physical condition was enigmatic. At times her problems seemed physical in nature, as with her back pain. Other times she was simply nervous, frightened, and emotionally fragile. If riding in a car she was afraid of having an accident. If Jim was climbing a mountain, she was afraid he'd fall off. If we children were playing outside, she was afraid we'd get lost. She was dominated by fear. Now, with the cooperation of well intentioned doctors, she kept a steady supply of powerful barbiturates at the ready, to ease the pain

There were things about Jim's lifestyle that might make any wife nervous, like this stunt on top of the Kissing Camels, Garden of the Gods, Colorado Springs. Jim was thirty stories high here, and he was no gymnast. Those 'ant-like' creatures down below are people.

or calm her jittery nerves. For Jim and we children, an indisputable nightmare had begun.

Shortly after Maxine's return from the hospital, Jim almost lost his beloved ranch. His own words:

Saturday morning, April 10, 1948, at our little log cabin headquarters at Star Ranch, the work hummed along just about as usual. Communications were being prepared for our staff, and for our entire mailing list. Final preparations were under way for a meeting at the ranch that afternoon. Just outside the work crew boys were beginning work on the new wing to the office building.

It was a beautiful spring morning, typical except for high velocity gusts of wind that kept whipping back and forth across the mountain in all different directions. About ten o'clock a large prairie fire started along the western edge of Camp Carson, several miles southeast of us. Propelled by a 52 mile-an-hour wind from the east, the fire came racing up the slope of Cheyenne Mountain toward the timber. It was apparent to all that our side of the mountain was exposed to great danger. Maxine talked to the sheriff and was told that the fire was out of control and that all available fire-fighting equipment was on the scene. She and some girls from our staff knelt in prayer in the living room of the Ranch House. When others of us came in a few minutes later, the wind had begun blowing the fire straight back in the direction it had come, and away from Star Ranch. All hearts were filled with thanks to the Lord.

Just then one of our staff girls came to the back door and beckoned to me. I could see she was alarmed. Hurrying out the door ahead of me, she pointed to a black column of smoke rising, it seemed, almost out of the front lawn, on the mountainside, directly toward our office in the woods. I ran across the lawn and up the office road. When I came to the path leading to the office, just fifty yards away, I stopped and took in one of the most terrifying sights I have ever seen.

Thick gray billows of smoke were pouring up all around the cabin area. Great sheets of flame were leaping out about the tops of the pine trees, 60 to 80 feet above the ground. Through the smoke and flashes of flame, I caught glimpses of the little headquarters building. Those flames seemed to melt down my heart. It was almost impossible to believe, standing there within a few feet of that roaring inferno, that our beautiful little office building with all its furnishings, national records, correspondence—everything that we used to carry on the work—was there going up in a blast of flame and smoke.

Even worse than that, as I stood there for just a few seconds, those flames raced through the tops of the trees toward the main Ranch buildings and our only road out. I knew in an instant that nothing but the power of God could ever save us from destruction—destruction that would ruin the Ranch work. This was no hysterical appraisal born of surprise and shock. It was the cold facts. Everyone at the Ranch that noonday felt that humanly there was no chance. The wind was fanning those giant flames in every direction at an unbelievable rate. The boys who followed me up to the cabin saw them jump across a hundred yard space and set the forest afire in an entirely new area in the space of fifteen seconds. We were helpless!

". . . Lord, with me abide:
When other helpers fail, and comforts flee,
Help of the helpless, O abide with me!"

I remember praying that as I ran to the car to take the family out of the fire area. There was one thing predominantly in my mind: "Lord, we have just felt our helplessness as we watched the progress of the fire two miles away. Now we are in desperate need with a fire right in our own grounds. No one can help but Thee!"

There were scores of prayers like that ascending from every Christian heart within sight of that terrifying column of smoke and fire. As I drove down the road to take my family to safety, we could see the flames, close now, leaping down the hillside towards the road.

I was compelled to stay at the ranch entrance on the highway. Other members of our crew soon started arriving. Together *we watched and prayed. I can be sure I am speaking for all when I say there was no peace or no power on earth to keep our hearts during those hours save the Lord. The mountain itself seemed to be bursting into flame. All kind of reports came from the fire area. Several different ones reported that all the buildings at the Ranch were destroyed and that the butane tank had exploded. In it all I was searching my heart, and once again I know I speak for the rest when I say that we were brought very close to Him and brought face to face with the very positive necessity of trusting implicitly in His way, regardless of the circumstances. The loss we felt we were sustaining was far and away too great to bear apart from Him.*

After awhile John Miller came, streaked with soot and sweat, grimy from hours of fighting the fire. I could not understand the broad smile on his face. Then he said, "Jim, you won't believe what I'm going to tell you. The headquarters office is not damaged." "But, John, I saw it going up in flames with my own eyes," I responded, as tears burst into my eyes. He said, "I know it Jim, I did too, but it didn't burn."

The feeling of relief, and the praise and inner peace and joy that welled up in me will not be properly described this side of heaven. One after another of those who later gave their eye witness accounts of the fire in the headquarters area, told of seeing the same thing that I had seen—giant flames roaring all over, apparently consuming the cabin, and yet not so. The cabin stood in this inferno with the fire licking at its walls on three sides, and DID NOT BURN!

I paced from the stone fence, surrounding our lawn area, straight across the road into the woods and found that the fire raged up to within thirty-five yards of the lawn and stopped. Where it stopped there was nothing to break a fire, just deep pine needles and scrub oak leaves such as you find in a forest area. But it stopped! All along the line it was that way. As the fire leaped towards the athletic area, it just stopped. As it raced toward the main dormitory building it just stopped. As it started down across the main Ranch buildings, it just stopped. The firefighters, the army officers, the Forest Service men, the Sheriff's crew, the city fire department—none could explain why it stopped as it did.

Saturday night fires kept breaking out but were kept under control. Some of our crowd prayed for rain or snow to remove the great danger. About 3:00 a.m. Sunday, it began to rain and was soon snowing hard. A Denver newscaster said, "An unusually heavy late snow has moved in from the Pacific Northwest. A strange thing about the storm is that it struck in Colorado Springs before it hit Denver." We did not consider this 'strange.' As I walked through the Ranch and watched the danger area through the evening, I was continually impressed with the word from the Psalm, "For the Lord God is a sun and shield." Truly He threw up a great wall of protection. We expect continually to sing the praises of God and to acknowledge His goodness and greatness for staying this terrible destruction and demonstrating beyond the peradventure of a doubt to every believing heart that He heard us in our time of need and met us in great power!

After this horrifying forest fire, Jim took Max on a mini-vacation to help calm her nerves. Together they selected a quiet little town on the western slopes of Colorado known as Glenwood Springs. They figured it would be a nice, peaceful place to spend a few days together, away from any problem or tension. Jim wrote:

5/9: Maxine and I left at 3:00 p.m. for Glenwood Springs after much hasty office work. We had a superb trip through my favorite part of the mountains and arrived at the Hotel Colorado at 9:30 p.m. where we quickly got bedded down in a nice big room.

5/10: Slept late this morning. Had a delicious breakfast with Maxine, and then I fooled around town getting car serviced. We went to Aspen for lunch. I was greatly impressed by the chair lift. Then we drove back to Basalt and went up the "Frying Pan" where Maxine camped as a child. Then on to Redstone and Crystal River Lodge. Came back to hotel at 6:30 p.m. for dinner at 8:00. Really a grand day!

5/11: Wonderful day with Maxine in Glenwood Springs.

On the 13th, Jim had to leave for Chicago. The vacation had been so peaceful, Maxine decided to stay in Glenwood for a few more days. "The day after Jim left," she recalled, "I decided to walk to the dime store to buy some material; I wanted to make some doll clothes for our girls. It was a peaceful, relaxing day, and I was feeling better than I'd felt in years. Pretty soon I heard a siren. People were scurrying around like ants. I walked across the bridge to the hotel without much concern, but when I arrived, I learned that the fire was in the oil and gasoline storage area only three or flour blocks away.

"Then it happened. The first of several storage tanks—KA BOOM!!! It was an explosion I can hardly explain—a bright flash, a thunderous roar, and a huge, billowing, mushroom-shaped cloud of black smoke and flame. I was almost blown over by the shock wave and heat. Then tank number two, fifty-thousand gallons of gasoline—FLASH—BOOM! The sky appeared to be on fire! It was like the town was being invaded, something hellish."

Gasoline storage tank explosions, May 14, 1948, in Glenwood Springs, CO. Jim had taken Maxine here to calm her nervous condition after the 1948 forest fire at Star Ranch.

71

"There were six or seven storage tanks, and they started going off one right after the other. People were screaming! We were all crawling around on the ground hoping to protect ourselves. It was terrifying!"

There hadn't been a day like that in Glenwood Springs ever before. Was Max simply in the wrong place at the wrong time? Excepting the tragic forest fire of 1994 a few miles outside of town, there has never been another tragedy of that magnitude in Glenwood Springs, and Maxine was there right in that hour. A sinister pattern of traumas had seemed to follow Jim and her ever since their union. It seemed that someone, somewhere, was bent on their destruction.

The attacks did not abate. Several months later, on a slow, peaceful, summer afternoon, an ear-splitting clap of thunder rumbled through Star Ranch. As the shock wave rolled by, everyone snapped to attention, momentarily stunned. The ensuing silence was interrupted by a young child's shriek, "A big spark hit my daddy, a big spark . . . !" Sue Rayburn, age eight, had seen it all.

Jim, Bud Carpenter, and Tom Henderson, a young camper, had all been struck by a savage bolt of lightning. All three were down; no one was conscious. As several staff ran to a telephone, others quickly carried the comatose bodies to a nearby cabin. Maxine recalled: "I never heard a deeper, louder clap of thunder; it really jolted me. I knew something was wrong; somebody was hurt. As fast as I could manage with the back brace I was wearing, I headed out the door and followed the source of the shouting. I had already learned that Jim was hit by the time I reached the cabin where they had taken him. Then someone hustled me away and accompanied me back to the house. Before long a strange man knocked on the door and asked to use the phone. I asked who he was and he replied, 'I'm the county coroner.' My heart turned over within me."

Tom Henderson, a young man attending Young Life camp for the first time, was killed instantly. Bud Carpenter, one of Jim's dedicated early followers and long-time staff man, was the first to regain consciousness. Jim, jolted to within an inch of his life, had burns on his shoulders and intense pain in his head and legs. The doctor thought him 'fortunate' to be alive. The lightning bolt, most interestingly, produced the longest interval in Jim's life without a migraine headache—five months. Jim's 1948 journal:

> 8/24: *About 5:00 p.m. as we were leaving the ball field, lightning struck, killed Tom Henderson and knocked out Bud and me. I woke up in the "Squirrel House" shortly before Dr. Karabin came. Had terrible pain in my head and legs felt peculiar. Very thankful to the Lord for sparing me. Can't help thinking a lot about Him leaving me here when I was so close.*

> 8/25: *In bed all day. Pain receding in a.m. Comfortable in afternoon and evening. Maxine's condition set back badly by this shock.*

> 8/26: *Able to get up today. Conducted a short service this evening. Maxine's state of mind very bad; her nerves are shot and she can't get any rest. I left about 10:30 p.m. for the plane.*

Within a six-month period, Jim had lost his wife to drugs, nearly lost his ranch, and barely survived a bolt of lightning. Fires and lightning would not keep him on the canvas, but the increasing weight of Maxine's illness was beginning to wear him down. By 1949 the stress was apparent. Jim's journal tells the story:

> 5/18: *Didn't go to Pueblo for club on account of Maxine's illness.*

> 5/29: *Very tough migraine began in afternoon, lasted all night. Maxine sick all day.*

> 5/30: *Up at 5:30 in spite of sleepless night. Migraine pain finally gone. A swell breakfast up on Strawberry Point with Orien and Roy. Came rushing right home after breakfast. Maxine sick and distraught all day.*

> 10/8: *A wonderful morning of prayer with the staff at headquarters. A hard afternoon—Maxine sick.*

> 10/9: *A wonderful class at church. A large crowd that was very attentive. Maxine very ill, spent rest of day with her. Feel very poor.*

10/19: Up all night with Ann. She had another bad asthma attack. Feel very beat up this morning. The health problems of family, weariness, and almost daily conflict with pain in my head is making serious inroads into my health and life. Good club in Pueblo tonight—I took the girls.

In spite of family problems and the pressures of leading a rapidly growing work, Jim's rapport with kids was keener than ever. His 1948-49 journals show this side of the story too.

4/23/48: Spoke at Queen Ann's High. Have spoken to eight or nine-thousand kids this week with great reception and cannot thank the Lord enough.

5/3/48: A grand club meeting tonight—110 kids—I spoke on I Peter 1:3-5 with such blessing I can never thank the Lord enough for it.

10/26/48: 187 at the Colorado Springs Club, average attendance for the fall is 170 per week.

4/5/49: A good club tonight with eighty-four kids—spoke on Luke 23.

10/18/49: Sick all night with migraine. Grand club meeting tonight, but more kids than we could possibly handle in the house, 139 plus . . .

10/3/49: A great high-school assembly for me in Yuma, Colorado. A wonderful reception from kids and faculty. Started club there tonight with sixty kids. Drove home after meeting. A great 22-hour day.

Jim was a master at handling the high school crowd. Kids tried everything imaginable to upset him, tease him, or gain the upper hand, usually to no avail. After one Young Life club in Texas, he found his car had been carried up some stairs and deposited on a stranger's porch. That Jim took such things in stride only increased his rapport with the pranksters. Their efforts to frustrate him were successful on occasion but he seldom let them know. On October

12, 1949, after a particularly difficult club in Pueblo, Colorado, he wrote:

A rather discouraging time with small crowd trying to go on John 2, but never got to the actual miracle.

A reformed heckler remembers: "At one club a friend and I were cutting up. During the singing we were tossing song books down on the head of another fellow. Finally Jim said, 'Sam, you're too noisy. Come down here and sit.' He indicated the front row among all the ninth-grade girls, and I was a junior. I was mad, yet I had so much respect for Jim that I went and sat there. I fumed; I glared; I stared at him. All I wanted was to get even and upset him. He continued club unruffled. He talked this time about successes in sports and popularity, how one could have all the things he wanted in high school, and still not have real life—contentment, joy, peace inside. Because I was so intent on trying to frustrate him, I actually heard what he was saying. 'The only way to know what real life has to offer is to know Jesus Christ.' I kept listening. He quoted 1 John 5:12: 'Whoever has God's Son has life; whoever does not have his Son, does not have life.' This really hit me, and I started thinking and evaluating what was going on in my own life. Many years later, here I am actively leading a Young Life club and a college leadership group. It's the closest thing to New Testament Christianity that I know of."

Other former roughnecks recall their impressions:

"I never saw anything that quite satisfied me until I saw Young Life . . . and I'd have to say until I met Jim. I was impressed with the club, but it was Jim's vision and compassion that impressed me most."

"I'd grown up in church and thought I understood what Christ was all about. Then I met Jim Rayburn. I could listen to him talk forever. He was funny, honest, and genuine—not at all what I was used to. Jim led me to an encounter with the Spirit of the risen Christ. Now I know the secret behind the man."

"I was never afraid to take my friends to Young Life. I knew they weren't interested in Christ, or anything related, but I also knew they had never met Jim. He was great; probably the best thing that ever happened in our high school was Jim's club."

Many have said, in jest, that they had their first spiritual encounter while hanging from Jim's mountain-climbing rope. There you'd be, clinging to a tiny spur of rock, your feet barely riding a narrow ledge, the wind threatening to blow you off the face of the cliff, and he would shout down, "Isn't this the most gorgeous place you've ever seen?" Once, in just such a situation with his daughter Ann, he shouted "Smile, honey, I want to take some good pictures." That was Jim all right! He relished life and believed God wanted us to experience it fully. His life was one of high adventure, and it would be impossible to separate him from the mountains he so loved. When Jim needed to go to "church," when he needed to hear his Savior's voice, his sanctuary of preference was the high country.

By the summer of 1949, the third season of operation of Star Ranch, Jim was secretly shopping for a second resort. His search for the right property took him to Buena Vista, Colorado, where he had spent many summers as a young boy. Together with Gus Hill, a close friend who shared Jim's concern for kids, he struck gold.

Byrd Raikes Fuqua, a visionary lady cut from the same cloth as Jim, had built what many considered the finest vacation resorts of their type in the country. The Byrd Colonies, as she named them, were composed of three units: Radio Spring Byrd Bath, the Alpine Lodge for Boys, and the Tin Cup Dude Ranch. Each unit was separate from the others, but all three were located in the heart of one of the most scenic spots in the State of Colorado. The great continental divide of mountains, the climate and the general surroundings equal anything to be found in the Alps or elsewhere in the United States. It's God's country, we'd say.

Old age and deteriorating health had forced Byrd Fuqua to sell her interest in these resorts. Upon transfer of ownership, the Radio Spring Byrd Bath became known as Chalk Cliff Lodge. Within the property boundary were the Hortense Hot Springs, the hottest in the state, having a temperature of 187 degrees F at the point of issue. Byrd, who had lost her sight during World War I years, claimed that bathing in these hot waters had restored her vision. Whatever the medicinal effects, these natural hot springs were of keen interest to Jim, who had bathed in these waters as a young boy. By the summer of 1949, Chalk Cliff Lodge was once again for sale; Jim was back on his knees asking God for the property. Wally Howard, one of the original team, recalls:

> "His faith had a daredevil quality about it. There were times when I could not decide if he was a man of God or just presumptuous, whether he was driven by ambition to serve Christ or to build his own empire. I wrestled with that, and I actually did not know. Sometimes I was angry because I thought him on an ego trip—then I would be humbled by the quantity and persistence of his faith, even after I questioned it."

Jim suspected that his interest in acquiring Chalk Cliff Lodge might be viewed as another irresponsible idea. Although he was reluctant to seek approval from his board of directors, God had laid it on his heart and he had to face the music. In September of 1949, he took Max and went to Chicago to see H. J. Taylor. Jim's journal tells what happened:

> 9/26: *Very weary this a.m., and very backward about doing what I felt I should—go see Mr. Taylor and Mr. Crowell about "Chalk Cliff." When I did the Lord rewarded me greatly with very refreshing fellowship with both men. A restful afternoon on the train with Maxine for home.*

> 9/27: *175 at my club tonight, at the ranch. Many new ones. Hard-to-handle crowd but went well. This is the end of a perfect trip. Maxine and I were greatly blessed in Chicago—all the way—and specially yesterday.*

> 11/17: *A very hard day.*

11/18: *Our day of prayer. It was hard for me to get into it much this time because of outside pressure (see 9/26). Then, the letter announcing a marvelous gift from the Crowell Fund toward the purchase of Chalk Cliff Lodge arrived. Thank the Lord!*

11/21: *Much time with Gus about Chalk Cliff. Have talked to John E. Mitchell and E. Wetmore. They agree to go ahead with effort to establish price and seek funds.*

One month and numerous miracles later, Jim and his Young Life work took possession of Chalk Cliff Lodge. The name was changed to Star Lodge, then later to Silver Cliff Ranch. The first kids' camp was held during Christmas vacation, 1949.

Jim's desire to have the classiest camps in the country was well on the way to being fulfilled, as both Star Ranch and Silver Cliff Ranch were prime properties in choice locations. More important was the obvious touch of God on the whole process of their acquisition. Jim was anointed, and God poured out His blessings upon his work. The more the blessings flowed, an unseen devil would come against Jim with increasing fury.

Here was a man who by his own admission felt 'too wound up,' a hard-working, hard-driving man who seemed ill-at-ease with restfulness and a slowed down pace. As he had deeply rooted Midwest values—Kansas stuff—being a hard worker was the only way. But first, he stayed up half the night talking with his Lord. Jim would say, "I am God's—God will lead me—He will not let go of me." And then Jim went, like a man possessed. God had to respond to the man. Jim was a sincerely friendly, warm, and attractive soul, who sought his Lord tenaciously. Can God remain silent with a man who gets on his knees as Jim did—and gets on his knees—and gets on his knees—and places himself into his Father's care? Of course not! Satan hated every minute of it, and he was relentless in his attacks upon we Rayburns.

Attack

IN 1950, Maxine was hospitalized once again for further treatment on her back. Early in the morning, January 17th, a nurse charged into her room and removed the radio. "Now that's a funny thing," Maxine recalled thinking, "Why would anyone want to take away my radio? I knew something had happened." About that time a cleaning person entered her room and made a remark about the terrible fire on Cheyenne Mountain. Max demanded that the radio be returned to her. The first thing she heard was a reporter close to the scene, broadcasting from a mobile unit. He said that Star Ranch was surrounded by fire and that all the people at the ranch were trapped. Horrified, Max headed for the nurse's station and demanded to be taken as close to the ranch as possible. She was escorted back to her room and in no time at all another nurse appeared carrying a vial of potent sedative. That was becoming Maxine's life, potent sedatives to mask her pains and calm her jittery nerves.

A city utilities crew had first noticed the fire at 1:00 a.m. just to the south of the Broadmoor Hotel's golf course. Workmen had been burning brush cleared from the area the day before and had gone home for the evening. A sixty mile-an-hour wind arose in the night, fanned the dying embers into flames, and blew them into dry scrub oak bushes surrounding the clearing. The gale-whipped flames spread rapidly to the southwest, taking the fire up the face of Cheyenne Mountain and directly towards Star Ranch.

Those of us living at the ranch will never forget this nightmare come true. It was the second major forest fire to threaten Star Ranch in twenty-one months. "Some man, we never found out who, called us about 4:00 a.m. and asked if we knew of the fire," said Harriet Johnson. "I said, 'No, what fire, where?' He said it was spreading rapidly, and it was headed in our direction. While I dressed our children, Charlie ran up to inform Jim. Charlie soon returned and we quickly loaded the kids into the car and headed down the mountain. We were confident that Jim and his children were right behind us.

Half a mile from the ranch, the quantity of smoke crossing the road made it difficult to see. Twice we ran off the road and at one point we were driving through tongues of flame. Miraculously, we made it out and pulled off the road to wait for those behind us. We waited and waited, but nobody came. It scared me to death. I was certain that those behind us, including Jim and his children, were trapped and probably burned."

By 5:00 a.m. volunteers were flocking into police headquarters. Colorado College men turned out in a body and were scattered throughout the fire area by those in charge. At Camp Carson, the large army base, every available soldier was called out. Fire fighting equipment and personnel were received from all over the eastern part of Colorado. The Colorado National Guard, Seabees, Soil Conservation Service, Naval Reserve, Forest Service, and many other organizations were on the scene.

Throngs of volunteers who came to police headquarters were hauled to the area in Army busses, dump trucks, police cars, the paddy wagon and moving vans from local companies. Officer Tom Hughes, who was hauling people to the fire in the police paddy wagon, said the wind was so strong he feared the vehicle would be blown over on its side.

"I'd heard the phone ring in the middle of the night," said Ann Rayburn, age thirteen at the time, "and I heard Daddy say, 'Oh, no, no!' Then he came to my room, shook me, making certain I was awake, and told me there was a big fire on the mountain. He asked me not to worry, to wake up Sue and Jim III, help them dress,

80

and wait in the living room for his return. He needed to leave and see what the situation was. He said, 'I'll be back, so please don't worry. You know I wouldn't leave you here. You must stay here where I can find you, no matter how frightened you are, you must not run.' Then he left, and the three of us huddled together in the living room. We could smell the smoke; we were frightened!

"After a while Daddy came charging through the door and said it was time to leave. He was visibly shaken, and just ran us to the car. Once outside, we were startled. The sky was bright red and the wind was unbelievable; it was difficult to breathe. Pine trees were exploding all around, sending flames hundreds of feet into the sky. I thought, 'I just don't believe this, I can't believe this.' It was horrifying!

"We had a memorable and frenzied trip down the mountain. Daddy said to roll up the windows as we were going to make a run for it, and that's exactly what we did. We literally drove through a tunnel of flame. What a horror-filled ride! Flare-ups would unexpectedly jump across the road right in front of us and we had no escape. We just kept driving through the flames; stopping was not an option.

"As soon as we were off the mountain, Daddy left us at a friend's house and headed back to fight the fire. I begged him not to go, but he loved the ranch, and couldn't be stopped. He was doggedly determined to save that property. I feared he'd sacrifice his life in the process."

The flames, now whipped by hurricane-force winds, quickly surrounded Star Ranch and were threatening to close the circle. "Our backs were to the walls of several buildings at the ranch," Gus Hill recalled. "The flames had gotten so close it was difficult to breathe, due to the heat, smoke, and gale-like winds. The only thing we could do in the strongest gusts was cover our faces and lie flat on the ground. Burning pine needles were blowing into the sides of some buildings and sticking there. It looked hopeless, as if the whole ranch would burn. There was no place to run and no place to hide. At one point, I heard a bulldozer coming in the back gate. As I looked up, the wind blew the driver off of the seat and rolled him over the side."

By late afternoon, it was apparent that the ranch had been spared. One cabin and the corral tack room had burned to the ground; one large dormitory lost its roof. The rest of the buildings were intact, even though burning mattresses were pulled from some of them. It was indeed another miracle that the ranch was still standing. No one could find a reasonable explanation for it.

It seemed fortunate that Maxine was not at home the morning of the fire. The event was altogether too traumatic for anyone with a serious nervous condition. But hearing that her family was trapped was a traumatizing experience in its own right, and only worsened her overall emotional state. Jim had no idea how to help her. It was a tangled web of physical and emotional problems which had baffled many a doctor and several psychiatrists. There were no simple answers.

Max was an enigma. She was sensitive to others, curious about the world she lived in, almost overly perceptive, and fun to be with. Her delightful personality would come and go like the tides, however. When feeling well, she was a gourmet cook, a talented artist, and a gifted writer. When not feeling well, as was usually the case, she was an altogether different person—depressed, pessimistic, frightened, and prone to long runs of heavy drug abuse. At these times she showed little interest in writing, painting, or life itself.

By 1950 her nervous state and deepening drug dependency were out of control. In a desperate search for help, Jim took her to Johns Hopkins University Clinic in Baltimore, Maryland, believed by many at the time to be the best facility available for those with drug dependencies. The people at Johns Hopkins offered no solution to Maxine's problem, but verified that the spinal surgery of 1948 had failed to provide her with any relief.

Jim never stopped trying to introduce his life-style to Maxine, in hopes that it would do for her what it had done for many others. He and his staff had no time for depression in their constant quest to see new places, meet new people, and discover new adventures. Few things, however, met with more failure than Jim's frequent attempts to get Max off her sickbed by converting her to his life of high adventure.

A case in point was the October, 1950, family vacation to Alaska. Dr. McClellan, a missionary doctor who had converted a World War II naval mine sweeper into a hospital ship for visits to the remote coastal hamlets of the last American frontier, had invited Jim to join him on a trip from Ketchikan to Sitka, with stopovers at such "famous" ports as Hydaburg and Klawock. The plan appealed to Jim as if he'd dreamt it up himself and he was excited to be taking his family.

"The people on that ship were very nice," Maxine recalled, "and they did their best to make that old mine sweeper as comfortable as possible. The doctor, who was also the captain, had a radio on board, which gave me some comfort, but my general impression was that no one really knew much about boating. They were just boat-crazy people having a good time and providing a much needed service.

"The whole thing scared me as our kids, especially Jim III, were so young. I was worried about the children running around on deck, so I made young Jim wear a life jacket at all times. Ann and Sue had to sleep at the other end of the boat from me, and I wasn't comfortable with that at all. Had there been an accident or fire, I was too far from the girls to be much help.

"One night at dinner, Dr. McClellan, a gifted surgeon, told us to scrub in the morning as he needed assistants in the operating room. We thought he was kidding us, but the next morning a nurse came and awakened us. 'They're ready for you in surgery,' she said. Jim and I just stood there, looking at each other.

"That was an experience. We finally scrubbed and reported to the operating room in our gowns. My job wasn't bad, but Jim's was difficult. He had to stand across from the doctor and do whatever he was told. Since this was a hernia operation, Jim was staring into the patient's stomach the whole time. At one point, he had both hands held out, palms up, and was holding something different with each finger.

"At the next little port, we met some friends of the doctor who had a submarine chaser; it was long, narrow, and fast. They invited us to go for a little trip, and wouldn't you know, Jim accepted. There was no radio, no radar, or anything on that boat, and something was always going wrong in the engine room; it was continually catching on fire. One couldn't go up on deck as there was no railing, just a flimsy rope. Jim and the children were in seventh heaven, but I had an ominous feeling.

"We went way out in the ocean, in one whale of a storm, and the boat's engine broke down. As they couldn't fix it, we were simply adrift out there. The storm was getting worse with each hour, and we were bouncing around like a cork. I never felt so helpless in all my life. All of us were huddled in the galley, and cans of food were flying across the room like missiles. We had no lights, as the boat's engine also drove the generator. The storm was so severe I thought we might capsize. I kept thinking, 'Dear God, how did I get in a place like this? And for what reason? For no darn good reason at all, just following Jim!'

"We spent the whole night, twelve long and dark hours, adrift in the Pacific Ocean, praying that we wouldn't roll over. It was the longest and worst night of my life. The next day they got the engine running well enough to limp back and meet the mine sweeper. That old tub never looked so good!

"On October 31, we docked at Klawock, Alaska. I wanted to get off the ship and take a walk. I was fed up with boats by then! As I got ready to go, one of the men came up and handed me a revolver. I said, 'You've got to be kidding.' He said, 'No, Maxine, if you go into those woods you've got to have a gun; we have bears and wolves out there.' I said, 'That's all right, I don't really feel like walking anyway.'"

By the time we reached Sitka, Maxine called it quits. Jim asked her to take me back to Ketchikan while he took my sisters farther north to view the glaciers. Travel from Sitka to Ketchikan was by boat or seaplane, and Max had no desire for another boat trip. Previously, she had no greater fear than that of flying, but with no other alternative, she consented; if given the option, she'd have preferred to make the trip by dog sled.

"That night adrift at sea," Maxine joked, "I had told God that if He'd get me out of there alive, I'd never get on anything dangerous again. First thing that happens, I'm faced with flying on a rickety old seaplane with a bush pilot. The morning of the flight, I was out

84

on the dock, as ready as I felt I could get. We waited and waited, but they couldn't get the engine started. I inquired of somebody, 'They can't start the engine?' He replied, 'No, and we've no idea why, It's the first time in twenty-three years it hasn't started.' I thought, 'My Lord, what do I do now?'

"Eventually another plane arrived; I felt better because the second plane had two engines. It was an awful flight, rough as could be. I was sitting there, sick as a dog, and everybody started eating lunch. I was so airsick I must have looked green, so the pilot came back to the cabin and jokingly offered me half his sandwich. They had quite a few laughs on my account, I'm sure."

In retrospect, incidents like these are humorous. At the time, however, Maxine's problems were no joke, not to the Rayburn family. Her fears weren't simply apprehension, as one might feel before riding a roller coaster. They were more like a wave of terror-inducing anxiety. Each anxiety attack drove her deeper and deeper into her private realm of escape.

Our problem with Maxine weighed like lead, and there were few with whom we could share this difficulty. The vast majority of the time, she was heavily sedated and couldn't even stand up, let alone walk, drive, or communicate. As Jim had become a big-name Christian leader, we were in the public eye and didn't dare let something of this magnitude become public. As a young child, this confused me. If Christ loved people like us, full of failures and weaknesses, then what did we have to fear from those who profess His name?

Frontier Ranch

ROUND UP LODGE was the prize property of the original Byrd Colonies, and an absolute showplace. It had been used exclusively as a summer camp for wealthy boys who came to spend the entire summer. Located on the slopes of Mount Princeton, it was only five-hundred vertical feet above Silver Cliff Ranch.

In August of 1950, eight months after the acquisition of Silver Cliff, Jim was invited to speak at Round Up Lodge for their twenty-fifth anniversary banquet. Max went with him so she could see the facility. "When the program was over," Max reminisced, "Jim and I were in the car, winding up that little road toward the corral. Jim said, 'Max, these folks don't know it yet, but this place doesn't belong to them anymore. I asked our Father for it this evening.'"

Although Jim was unaware of it, Cy Burress and Jerry Kirk, two kids on the Silver Cliff Ranch work crew, had stumbled upon the property while on a hike and were also praying that Round Up Lodge would someday be Young Life's. One month later, Dr. Marguard, the owner of Round Up, was informed by his doctor that a heart condition would necessitate his avoiding high altitude; his lodge would have to be sold. Shortly thereafter, Ted Benson informed Jim of an ad in the *New Yorker* for a half-million-dollar boys' ranch in the Colorado Rockies. Investigation confirmed the ad was referring to Round Up Lodge.

Jim, Cy, and Jerry had prayed for a miracle. How thrilled Jim would have been if his staff had shown the faith and vision of those two work-crew kids. But when it came to supporting Jim's dreams, his staff seldom got on board. Jim was usually doubted, and this was a constant drain upon him over the years. Because of this pattern, Jim did not tell his staff about Round Up Lodge until he'd met with the board of directors. But the pressure of asking the board to approve this latest venture brought on yet another migraine. What if these men turned thumbs down? What would he do if caught between the Spirit's leading and a contradictory directive from the board? Jim described the meeting in his journal entry of January 29, 1951:

> Arrived Chicago 2:45 a.m. with developing headache. In bed at LaSalle Hotel before 4:00 a.m. Up at 9:00 a.m. Breakfast with Gus and Millie Hill. Met Hathaways, talked to Frank Taylor, and went to board meeting .

> A great meeting! I was bowled over in the end when they voted to approve the expansion project and authorized me to seek the funds. Although very ill with headache I went out to see Coleman Crowell and he took me to the train. Bitter cold in Chicago (8 below zero). Left at 7:15 for Memphis, Tennessee. Had to give myself a shot at 5 p.m.

Jim was so thankful and excited one would think that his board had agreed to purchase this magnificent property. All they had actually done was authorize him to seek the funds. As Jim's train left Chicago, he wrote Maxine the following letter:

> Monday Evening, 1/29/1951
> En Route Memphis

> Dearest Maxie,

> This is your birthday! I feel sad because you will think I forgot. I am writing to let you know, even though late, that I have thought of you and remembered your birthday many times since early this morning. The Board meeting was one of the very

best we have ever had. Just before adjournment at 4:30 p.m. I told them about Round Up Lodge. They were bowled over! And they, in turn, bowled me over. To my utter amazement, Mr. Taylor said that the board should authorize me to contact wealthy donors and large foundations for the money to buy Round Up. There was an enthusiastic, unanimous vote authorizing me to seek the funds. Claude, Gus, and I were naturally overjoyed! Honey, although we haven't got Round Up by a long shot, it was an amazing vote of confidence, and further evidence to me of the Lord leading.

I had dinner with Coleman Crowell; he stayed in town just for that. I had such pain and nausea, I just sipped at a bowl of broth and talked to Coleman until train time. That's the way the day went—busy, and complicated by that terrible pain, but a wonderful day!

I thought of you many times. It doesn't seem possible that you are thirty-nine. I always think of you as a little girl, like when I met you. When you're well enough to be your true self, you're still as sweet, desirable, and beautiful as you have always been. Since the first time I saw you in the Concordia Church, you have been the only girl I ever wanted. I've loved you and wanted you ever since that night. The years of illness have made it seem to you, at times, like that wasn't so, but it is.

My life was made rich by your love, especially in those blessed first years—in school—at Concordia—even at Newton , and our belated honeymoon in Colorado. Best of all were the years at Chama, Douglas, Dos Cabezas, and Clifton, when you wanted so little and gave so much. I've thousands of precious memories that you gave me, of things so small you would doubt I even remember them. I couldn't have had those memories if you hadn't loved a guy starting out the hard way, at a job he didn't know how to do. I remember years when we had less materially than ever, yet we never lacked a thing, as we were so happy with each other.

Besides a million other joys, you've given me the sweetest kids in all the world. Each one of them means more to me than everything else in the world combined. So remember, darling girl,

I love you! I'll bet you'll be able to pass for thirty-nine for at least another fifteen years, and ten times easier than Jack Benny can.

Yours,
Jim

Coming home was not such a warm experience as Jim's letter would imply. He and Max did well from a distance, but things were often strained when he returned. Jim would arrive and not be greeted with so much as a hug; usually, Max wouldn't even go to the door. This absence of physically expressed warmth and affection was a difficult rejection for Jim, for he truly loved Max in spite of her deepening problems.

Two weeks after the Chicago board meeting, Jim informed his staff of his plans to purchase Round Up Lodge. Some wondered if he was sane. All staff salaries, including his, were low; survival seemed always to be a day-to-day affair. How could Jim possibly think of acquiring that amount of money? But Jim's faith was the product of the Spirit; he simply didn't limit God. Jim's journal of 1951 tells of the purchase:

2/21: A grueling but wonderful day. Arrived in Chicago at 9:00 a.m. Had meeting of trustees at Continental Bank. We went all afternoon! Talked about Round Up Lodge from every angle. It did not look too favorable when we broke up, but the Lord gave me a wonderful peace! After being violently ill, I got a good night's rest. Had to have a shot for headache—first time since the board meeting on 1/20.

2/22: What a day! This is the day the trustees voted to give $100,000 for the expansion project. What can I say? This is one of the greatest things the Lord ever did for me. And truly he did it all! Without him, it would be folly to attempt such things. Now to follow him for the next step.

2/24: The praise, thanks, peace, and joy that I am experiencing nearly overwhelm me! Never has the dear Heavenly Father permitted me, in His Grace, to experience so much tangible evidence *of his gracious dealings and sovereign leading in my life, as in these last days. Left Colorado Springs at 5:45 a.m. Met dear friends C.H. and Hazel at Denver station. Had a precious hour with them, rejoicing together about all that is happening. Then these dear people pledged $50,000 to the Expansion Project! What can I or anyone say? They further said that if their foundation can be formed, they will give $100,000 this year and next! A total of $200,000 in two years that they hope to give! Just had time to grab the California Zephyr at 8:40 a.m.*

3/20: Today was the day! We closed the deal for Round Up Lodge after a long, hard day with Dr. Marguard. What can I possibly say? The Lord is so wonderful and has done such a super, abundant thing for us. I want always to PRAISE and THANK HIM! Talked to Crowell trustees, also to Mr. Wetmore, Mr. Weyerhauser, Mr. Mitchell, and Mr. Gillis. All agreed we go ahead! A great spirit of oneness! Mrs. Paulsen made a splendid pledge today to take us over $300,000.

Less than seven months had passed since Jim had told Maxine that Round Up Lodge would soon be in his hands, because he had asked the Father for it that evening. At that time, this beautiful facility was not up for sale, nor did the owner have any intention of selling it.

Those who had watched the miraculous acquisition of these beautiful resorts were amazed. It seemed as if Jim's next trick would be to walk on water. Everything the man envisioned, no matter how absurd it seemed, came to pass. Star Ranch, Silver Cliff Ranch, and Round Up Lodge—now Frontier Ranch—had all been acquired in the short span of four years. They were all showplaces indeed, some of the fanciest camps in the country.

People who had scoffed at Jim found themselves with "egg on the face." Wally Howard says, "We questioned his wanting to get the camp properties, but every time, we enjoyed them as much as he did. Sometimes we felt embarrassed that we were receiving all these benefits that none of us were qualified to visualize or to go out and get. I decided that I would never again question Jim's telling us the Lord was laying it on his heart to get more property."

Frontier Ranch was truly special to Jim. It was his idea of God's sanctuary, an awe-inspiring, mighty expanse of majestic beauty. Located on the backbone of the great continental divide and nestled in the splendor of cathedral-like cliffs towering one thousand feet above her, Frontier Ranch became Jim's lover. She restored him, rebuilt him, and sent him off to battle with a soft kiss. His residence there was known as the Lookout, and more than any other place he considered it home.

A corner of the living room in the 'Lookout' at Frontier Ranch.

Those summers spent in the Lookout were the happiest days of Jim's life. The awesome beauty of the place seemed an appropriate match to Jim's inspiring faith and life-style. It was wonderful to see my father so fulfilled. Life had thrown a lot of problems in his direction, and the Lookout seemed to be God's way of providing him a special refuge.

A former staff man recalls: "Jim should have lived there year around. There was such a warm, special aura to the place when he was in residence. It's almost like the Lookout misses Jim as much as he would later miss her. The place seemed to be alive, bustling with adult guests, or the international exchange students he always invited up for cantaloupe, filled with ice cream and smothered with freshly picked raspberries."

At Frontier Ranch, Jim introduced thousands of kids to one of his favorite sports, snow sliding. High in the majestic Rockies, at an elevation of roughly 13,000 feet, he would find a snow cornice, a place where the prevailing winter winds blowing across a high ridge created an overhang, or ledge, of snow. The ideal cornice would have a twenty to thirty-foot vertical drop onto a steeply inclined snow field.

After finding the best location, Jim would gather the crowd, give a brief set of instructions, and slowly start inching out on the cornice while everybody watched. When the snow could no longer support his weight, he simply disappeared through a small hole, screaming and hollering all the way. It was a weird experience if you were following him and didn't really understand what was happening, since there was no way for those left standing on the ridge to see below. Jim's fate remained a question mark. One had only the memory of his scream fading away as he dropped a thousand feet into the valley below, and the small hole through which he'd disappeared.

The most difficult position was to be the next in line. Not knowing for certain if Jim was dead or alive, person number two would reluctantly inch toward the edge of the cornice. Eventually, when he was about to change his mind, the snow would give way—whoosh! Another scream, another small hole, and the third person in line now stood there alone, an apprehensive look upon his face.

93

Frontier Ranch as it appeared in 1951 when Jim acquired it for Young Life. The 'Lookout' is in the background. With exception of the 'Lookout,' all the buildings pictured here, as well as the pool, have been rebuilt.

1952, excited kids at Frontier Ranch, leaving for a day in the high country and a taste of 'snow sliding.'

As Jim explained to many a skeptic, it was all a matter of physics. There was little shock to one's body after the fall, as the snow field below the cornice was extremely steep. After hitting the snow, one could slide a thousand feet down the mountain in thirty seconds. The real danger was the emotional trauma felt by those who didn't share Jim's zest for adventure—that, and the ever present sensation of nearly freezing to death.

Snow sliding was a thrilling sport. Most kids who tried it became instant enthusiasts, making as many trips down the mountain as they had strength for. Overcoming beginner's fear served to make the whole experience more exciting.

We used to return from the snow slides with Jim driving in front, and all the trucks and buses, loaded with kids, strung out behind. At one point, he'd pull over to the side of the road and the whole caravan would come to a halt, waiting for Jim to reveal a problem. Then, just like a madman, he'd go running across the river. Sometimes he'd trip and fall, and come up dripping and spluttering, waving for everyone to join him. It must have confused many a

On the way to the snow slides, at St. Elmo, Colorado, Vickie Ekdahl and Pitt McGehee on the cable over Chalk Creek.

tourist, or fisherman, when three-hundred kids emptied from the buses and ran pell-mell into the ice cold river.

Another of Jim's loves was exploring old mines. He had graduate credits in geology and was well aware of which mines were safe and which were not. There were few things he loved more than taking a group of kids deep into the belly of the earth to show them the ins and outs of gold and silver mining.

Jim's main love was mountain climbing. Dr. "Chubby" Andrews: "Jim was one of those fellas peculiarly built for mountain climbing, with his sort of bow legs, and his feet that seemed to grab hold of the side of a mountain, like a billy goat climbing right on up to the peak. There wasn't anything he was afraid to tackle.

"That rascal Rayburn said, 'Chub, I know a lake up there on top of the mountain that's just loaded with trout. You bring your rod and we'll catch em.' But he just wanted me to hike up that moun-

An early morning Wrangler's Breakfast at Jim's Colorado Ranches. It seems he either had the horses or the campers fording streams with great regularity.

tain with him! It was a beautiful place, but I didn't catch a fish. He had a way of making it fun, regardless. His enthusiasm just swept you into whatever he had in mind . . . . It captivated you."

When mountain climbing, snow sliding, four wheeling, camping, or exploring mines, few could match Jim's rapport with kids. Nor could anyone present Jesus Christ to young adults more effectively than he could. But for all his gifts, Jim could be somewhat unbending in his viewpoints, much like his mother had been.

At the ranches, for example, Jim enforced a nap. After lunch, from the moment you walked out the dining-hall door, it was Silence! You couldn't say a word. Just go back to your cabin and lie down for one solid hour. For those kids with red blood in their systems that was the longest hour of the day!

So much of Christ's message deals with relationships, and few could present that message like Jim, yet his own inability to be more flexible in little things like the nap issue, would sometimes drive a wedge between Jim and some of his staff. Jim set very high standards for himself in everything he approached, and he expected the same from his people. If a meal was late being served, or something not done the way he wanted it, he'd sometimes overreact, and give the one responsible a tongue-lashing that he'd later regret. This tendency was not his most endearing trait, but then, the Rayburn boys had never been known for their timidity.

The emphasis received in childhood to be on top, to make people proud, to live a life beyond reproach had made it difficult for Jim to deal with criticism. Censure was a very personal thing for him; to be criticized was to be disliked, and that hurt him deeply. "I remember an early staff conference at Star Ranch," Norm Robbins recalled, "where Jim broke down and wept, right in front of the whole group. The reason? He'd heard talk about his being difficult to get close to. It just wiped him out!"

Underneath Jim's stern exterior lived the heart of a puppy. Outwardly he could give the impression of self-sufficiency, almost

Jim felt it was a crime to bore people with the Gospel. He not only kept it interesting, he was a laugh riot. To this day, his Young Life work retains his emphasis on humor. Laughing plays a big role in any and all work that Jim inspired.

cockiness. In his heart, however, he was deeply aware of his short-comings, as is seen in these journal entries:

> "Oh, how I long to do better work for the Lord. He is so wonderful, and I'm such a stick at presenting Him."

> "I preached on John 9 and as far as the people were concerned they were very cordial and complimentary and I know the Lord used me but I must confess that I was quite disappointed with myself for this day—there is so much more I could be by His Grace."

> "The blessed Lord gave me an unusual experience of perfect liberty in the pulpit, and, I believe, gave a message that went home to people's hearts. I feel most happy about today and have much warm gratitude to God for all that He has done. It must be ALL of Him. I certainly have nothing to offer."

> "Fine day but too much failure in my own personal relationship to the Lord."

> "I gave a Gospel Message and eight young people of high school age accepted Christ as their Savior! Three splendid fellows made complete surrender of their lives to Him. Wonderful morning! I didn't have the liberty I wanted but the Lord blessed. The people fell on my neck! How can I ever measure up to these dear people's expectation of me?"

> "I was privileged to speak to two-thousand students in three different assemblies. But tonight I couldn't get going. Tried to speak on I John 2:2 but didn't succeed. Just pray that the Lord will be able to use it though. Oh how people need to be stirred by the Word and how I hate to muff opportunities that He gives to me."

At the ranches during the summer, many of Jim's followers were awed and strengthened by Jim's commitment to prayer. When discouragement plagued them, Jim would get a few men together and say, "We're gonna get the horses and ride up Mt. Princeton to the saddle." He would take four or five men at a time, and he'd take them up there to pray, all night. "First time I went I couldn't believe it," said a staff man from this era, "I'd camped out before, but pray all night? I didn't know what to think! It was easy to stay awake; I was cold! We'd rustle up some hot coffee and just pray. Words fail to express what those times came to mean."

On other occasions, Jim called his people together for three days of prayer. A staff member recalls: "At the time I thought, 'How in the world can I spend three days praying? This is crazy!' But we did, and Jim kept us right at it. He didn't mess around. He'd say, 'Well, boys, we're here to pray. We're here to pray.' Those turned out to be some very special times."

While in summer residence at the Lookout, Jim's creative hosting of adult guests launched his work into a new era. From governors and senators to the popcorn vendor at the local rodeo, the great and the small came to taste his hospitality. A gracious host, he was well known for loading visitors into his convertible or jeep and disappearing for the day in his beloved mountains. Exposing guests to the kids, the facilities, the program, and the 'high country' was his avocation. This constant exposure to new people in every walk of life moved Jim into a higher realm of thinking and planning. In a sense, he was out-growing his own people.

Message of Life in a Mortuary

BY 1952, Jim's Young Life club in Colorado Springs was drawing from three-hundred to five-hundred kids per week. And this in an era when most churches were fortunate to have a dozen kids in their high school program! Finding a meeting place adequate for four-hundred people was no small problem, as Jim refused to hold his meetings in a church. The solution? The Swan Funeral home.

Loud music poured forth from the parlor room at the local mortuary every Tuesday night at 7:30. One of the favorite songs contained the line, "He lives, He lives, He walks with me, He talks with me . . . ." Legend has it that passing pedestrians were more than a little alarmed by such music emanating from a mortuary.

What magic brought out such numbers of typically uninterested kids to hear about Jesus Christ? What did Jim tell them; why would they come? Let's 'listen' in . . .

Almost everybody's heard about Jesus Christ. It would be hard to imagine that any rational person in the United States of America didn't know the name of Jesus Christ. The reason? It's probably the most common curse word in all the world! One of the names of the Savior is used more often than any other name for cursing. Isn't that a terrible thing? Most people never stop and think how incongruous that is. Jesus never hurt anybody; he

Jim's Colorado Springs Young Life Club in the Swan Funeral Home parlor. There were 467 kids on this night—265 of them did not fit in the picture, taken in 1952.

never did anything wrong. You can scrutinize his life as carefully as you want to, but you cannot find anything that isn't admirable.

Jesus was the kind of a man we men would like to be and can't be, 'cause we haven't got the guts. He was the kind of man you girls would like your man to be, but he'll never be that. He won't be as courageous, he won't be as gentle, he won't be as compassionate, he won't be as loving, he won't be as tender, he won't be as manly as Jesus Christ. And yet if you hit your finger with a hammer or want somebody to think you're real tough, you usually blurt out the name of Jesus, or Christ. In some connection, in some dirty way, you use the dearest name that ever was.

That's what your gang does at your school, isn't it? And I'm not picking on just your school. Saturday night I'll be talking to kids in Philadelphia, I won't even know what school they go to, but I can say it just as easily, because it happens in every school. If you want to peddle some dirty gossip, or tell a dirty lie, or defame somebody's character, or do something that's ugly, you almost always use the name of Jesus Christ in connection with it.

Did you ever think of that? Right down at your school! Come and tell me if it isn't so; you'll break a record. I've told several hundred-thousand kids, "That's what they do at your school, isn't it?" Nobody ever comes and tells me, "Jim, you're wrong, they don't do that at our school. Nobody ever says bad things about girls at our school. Nobody uses the name of Jesus or Christ. Why, we wouldn't think of doing that!" Not one! You see, I'm so right I don't have to worry about anybody saying that. I'd be shocked clean outa my shoes if somebody came and said I was wrong, 'cause I've been right for so long. But it's terrible to be so right, so right about such a terrible thing.

Tomorrow when you hear somebody blurt out a bunch of filthy conversation, and it has the name of the Savior mixed up in it, you probably won't think much about it. We're used to ugly things. We've got dirty insides. That's why I'd hate to have to be good enough for God. I've got dirty insides. We've all got dirty insides!

We don't put God in the right place. We don't respect human life and human personality, or we wouldn't lightly mix up the dearest and sweetest things with the ugliest things. No real person would, man or woman. We don't get things in their right place. The only people, I believe, that ever get 'em in the right place—get right and wrong, good and bad, things that count and things that don't count, things that build up and things that tear down—the only people that ever get things in the right place are the people who have Jesus Christ in the right place.

There's a mysterious thing that happens when you get properly related to Jesus Christ through this trusting business, believing on Him the way the Bible says. Then something happens inside of you, something God does. You don't have to struggle with it. It comes from God. It makes new life because it actually is a new life. It makes new life possible for you because it's a new life in you.

I want to take three witnesses tonight, three of my great heroes, three of the greatest men who ever lived—Peter, John, and Paul. They weren't great at all until they met Jesus Christ! He made 'em great! They're perfect illustrations of how Jesus Christ can take common, ordinary people, like you and me, and make them great. Take Peter, for instance. He was a "blunderbuss" sort of a fellow—probably a loudmouth, a fellow who spoke first and thought later. What he said was usually wrong. He was a fisherman. Doesn't take too many brains to be a fisherman. Even I can catch fish. There wasn't anything famous about him; he was just a common, ordinary, workin' boy, that's all. One day Jesus came by, stopped Peter, and had Peter come with him. I'll leave it with you, when you get interested in history, to find somebody that made a greater mark than Peter. I know two or three, but Peter stands up at the head of the human race as one of the greatest men ever produced. You'd have never heard of him if it hadn't been for Jesus Christ! Never woulda heard of him!

Now John was a friend of Peter—he was in the same business. From the nickname Jesus gave him, Son of Thunder, I wouldn't be surprised but what John was a loudmouth too. That may have been a loudmouth mob down there on the Sea of Galilee. You can't tell, but I kinda believe they were. They were always on the sea, there weren't too many people around, so they could make all the noise they wanted.

Now, John. You don't know beans about John, his background and all. Nobody else does either. John was the son of Zebedee. Yeah, but who ever heard of Zebedee? We wouldn't even know that John was the son of Zebedee if it wasn't for John; Zebedee never did anything! All in the world he gets credit for is being John's old man. Just think that over for a minute—you may come up with something, John wouldn't be anybody but the son of Zebedee, and Zebedee wasn't anybody that people ever heard of, if it hadn't been for Jesus Christ. Who is John now? Because he met Jesus Christ, he's one of the greatest loved, one of the most impressive, and one of the most majestic figures in the whole human race. You can go to great cathedrals and find them named after John—the Cathedral of St. John the Divine. Now he'd just faint if he'd heard 'em calling him Saint John the Divine, 'cause he was just a common, ordinary boy like you and me. Only thing is, he met Jesus Christ, and Jesus Christ made a wonderful person outa him. He'll do that for you, too. But John was no more a saint than I am. Nobody calls me Saint Jim.

Now Paul wasn't a nobody; Paul was a somebody, that is, in a certain circle. These two boys, Peter and John, they were just nobodies; they were just kinda bums down there on the Sea of Galilee, catching fish and horsin' around—talking a lot. But Paul, he was a leading citizen of Damascus. Now I'll ask you just one question. Outside of Paul, just name for me one other leading citizen of Damascus . . . [pause] You can't do it! Paul was a prominent fellow; he was a leading man in the synagogue. He was a very religious sort of person. But we'd have never heard of Paul if it hadn't been for Jesus Christ. All the other leading citizens of Damascus have long since gone down the drain. We can hardly remember where Damascus was, and we wouldn't know about Damascus at all if it wasn't for Paul. Paul put Damascus on the map. But he wasn't great, great enough to stand at the head of the human race, until Jesus Christ came into his heart.

Jesus Christ, the Savior. He makes life work. Now a lot of you say, "Oh yes, I believe in Him all right," and then you go on acting like you don't. John says that if you say you love God, and hate somebody, you're a liar. You see? He wipes out this idea that you can be a Christian simply by saying, "Oh yes, I've done this and I've done that; oh yes, I belong to the church; oh yes, I believe in Jesus Christ." A person who has really put his trust in Jesus Christ has a new life. It came to him from God; he's not a Christian because of anything he's done.

Peter, John, and Paul—if you trace the secret of their success, you'll find the reason they were great was that they saw what Jesus Christ had done for them. You can't pick up a Bible without seeing that. For—that's just a common little old preposition, but it's also one of the biggest words in the language. I don't care if you belong to every church in town, if you're the nicest boy or girl in your high school; I don't care if your name is above reproach, if you don't know the meaning of for, if you don't know what Jesus Christ has done FOR you, then you're not a Christian, and you're kiddin' yourself if you think you are! You don't know what life is all about, and you haven't even started to live yet. You're messing around with some kind of counterfeit article, 'cause life begins with Christ. What do you believe Jesus did for you? All the people I know that have been changed, like Peter, John, and Paul, believe one thing—I don't care whether they're Catholic, Jewish, or Protestant; I don't care what color their skin is; I don't care how much education they've had—they all believe that Jesus Christ did something for us that we could never have done for ourselves.

Jesus did somethin' tremendous for me, so much that when I think of it the teardrops start; so much that I'll never be able to thank Him; so much that it wouldn't make any difference if I never had another happy moment, if I could just please Him, and honor Him, and show Him how thankful I am. He suffered for me, the just for the unjust, to free me from the curse of death, and give me a new life.

I'll close with a tragic and fascinating illustration from the Gospels. You know the day they took Jesus Christ into Pilate's

Hall, into that crazy kangaroo court with all those trumped-up charges which nobody believed, and actually got a death sentence pronounced on the only man in the world that never deserved any punishment. When all this happened, there was at the same time a man in death row waiting for his execution. He had one chance to be set free. There was a strange Jewish custom that the Romans observed, that anybody who was sentenced to death, prior to the feast of the Passover, was eligible to be set free. The Jewish religious leaders could pick out any person guilty of a crime that had the death penalty, and they'd set him free, as a part of the celebration of the feast.

The man in jail was named Barabbas. Barabbas was a murderer; he had been in an insurrection, and he was guilty of murder during the insurrection. He was in death row, and he was about to be executed. The chief priests and the elders persuaded the crowd that they should ask freedom for Barabbas and destroy Jesus. The governor said, "Which of the two will you that I release unto you?" And they all said, "Barabbas!" Pilate said to them, "What then shall I do with Jesus?" And they yelled, "Crucify him!" You and I are members of the same human race that did that; they had a choice between a murderer and Jesus Christ, the Savior. We have the choice, we human beings. Whom will you have? Barabbas or Jesus?

Now don't you ever stop and think, "I wouldn't have done anything like that." Do you know who those people were? Those were some of the finest people in Jerusalem. Those were the respected, trusted, religious leaders of the city. Anybody who puts himself in the place where Christ is supposed to be, anybody who says that he is good enough for God and doesn't acknowledge that he needs Jesus Christ, is guilty of yelling "crucify him" or yelling for a murderer to be saved, instead of Jesus. All right! The murderer was set free. Just look at ole Barabbas, cringing in death row, shiverin' and shakin' and wonderin' when they are gonna knock on his door. And just think of him as the clamor comes down the hall, and the door is jerked open, and the soldiers kick him out. "Get outa here—you're set free—they chose you to be set free. They had somebody who was really somebody to free, and they chose you instead, you dirty bum."

They took Jesus, led him up to a place outside the city called Golgotha, the place of the skull—dirty, ugly name. They took Him up there, pounded spikes in His hands and feet, and hung Him on a cross to die. God says, "for you, for me. "Paul says, "He died for me." Peter says, "He suffered for me." John says, "God gave Him for us." There was one fellow in town that day who really understood what that meant.

Barabbas was free; he coulda been there. If he was there, I can almost see him, lookin' up at that cross, lookin' at the one he didn't know. Jesus had been beaten, He'd been spit on, He'd had a crown of thorns pressed down on His head, He was blood smeared, He was such a beat-up mess He didn't even look like a human. But there He hung, up there on the cross, suspended between heaven and earth, for you and for me. All the weight of His dear body hanging on those ugly spikes, and this Barabbas, walkin' around the cross. What do you suppose he was thinking?

Barabbas was the one man in Jerusalem who knew what it meant for someone to die in his place. I like to stand in his shoes and look up at the Savior. Jesus was bloody, beaten by men of my own race, religious men, well-reared men like I was, men who thought they were good enough for God and could get along without a Savior. And I want you kids to know, I don't see how you can leave him out. I don't see how you can act like you don't love Him. I should think He'd make so much difference to you, you couldn't stand it, and you'd rush to thank Him for what He's done. But you can't walk out of here saying, "Jim's right, I'm going to be a better person," 'cause that's not what I'm saying.

This would be a good time for you to pray, a real good time. "Well, Lord, I just never have done anything about this, I never have settled it. Jesus died for me all that long time ago, and He's given me sixteen or seventeen years of good life on this earth, and I've never given Him one thing. I've never even thanked Him for dying for me."

"But as many as received Him, to them gave He power to become the sons of God, even to them that believe on His name."

See? If you believe this, really believe it, way down deep in your heart, He'll bring you new life, He'll make you right with God. He'll give you a wonderful, wonderful treasure. Jesus said, "Behold, I stand at the door and knock; if any man hear my voice and open the door, I will come in. You got ahold of the handle— you wanna open the door? Jesus Christ will come in as soon as you open the door. He's there. He's there knocking—He's there waiting.

Malibu Resort

CHAPTER *11*

A WONDROUS adventure was initiated in January of 1952 when Jim met the Campbells of Seattle, Washington, during a reception at the home of Add and Loveta Sewell. Jim and Elsie Campbell's son, Jim Jr., had been a guest at Star Ranch the previous summer and had returned home 'leaking steam' about Young Life. When the Campbells were invited to meet the man who'd started it all, they enthusiastically accepted.

Jim Campbell was the owner of a Seabee (a private seaplane) and flying was his passion. Add Sewell, one of the Young Life pioneers from Dallas Seminary, had even asked him to fly over some property in the San Juan Islands to check on its suitability for a Young Life property. Mr. Campbell didn't feel the San Juan acreage was right, but knowing of Jim's interest in acquiring another kid's resort in the Northwest, he mentioned, tongue in cheek, that Young Life ought to acquire the Malibu Club, a fabulous million-dollar resort where he had been a guest, up the inland waterway beyond Vancouver. He mentioned that it was for sale.

Even though Jim Campbell had been joking, Rayburn's interest peaked. After speaking at the University Presbyterian Church that evening, Jim went straight to the Campbell's house to ask more questions and view some pictures of this remote resort. Elsie Campbell put it this way, "As we talked and saw more pictures Jim got almost high in his excitement. It was one a.m. before he decided to leave. He said he'd be returning to Seattle in March to see the NCAA basketball finals, and wondered if my husband, Jim, could fly him in to see Malibu. My husband told him he'd be happy to fly him there but didn't think there would be any purpose to the trip."

Elsie Campbell, in her book called *Malibu*, recalled, "March rolled around and the trip materialized. On March 26th, 1952, Jim flew Rayburn, Add Sewell, and me up to Malibu. The flight was smooth and beautiful. Both Jim and Add were almost overcome with the beauty and grandeur of the scenery. As we crossed over Patrick Point my husband pointed out the buildings of Malibu ahead. I will never forget Rayburn saying, 'There is Young Life's next property.' I also remember how Add, my husband, and I sort of laughed—in an embarrassed way—but said nothing. He was just a dreamer we thought.

"It was an unforgettable experience as we led Jim on a tour of the whole complex. When we came to each building he very simply stated what Young Life would use it for. He never said, 'If we get it,' but rather, 'This will be the boy's lodge, this we will have to enlarge, this we will use for such and such . . .'

"After clearing his throat, my husband timidly and half jokingly said to Mr. Rayburn, 'It sounds like you think Young Life is going to get this place. They only want one-million dollars for it, you know.' One would have had to know Rayburn to fully appreciate his response. He turned towards my husband, pulled himself up to his full height, and looked him up and down. And in that slow drawl Rayburn said, 'If the Boss wants us to have it, we'll have it.' With that he turned away and continued the tour. By now my husband and I were sure we had a nut in tow. Oh, ye of little faith!

"During the unforgettable day of flying into Malibu, touring the grounds, and our flight out, my husband and I, and I'm sure Add Sewell, were nearly in shock over Rayburn's positive attitude about Young Life acquiring and using Malibu. Not only did the huge dollar sign keep getting in our way, but how on earth would the number of people required to operate such a place, and the number of campers required to fill it, ever be flown or boated into this isolated spot? The human mind cannot comprehend the ways of an all powerful

God, and few of us ever have the childlike faith that God asks us to have. Jim Rayburn had it and it seemingly never wavered."

That night, March 26, 1952, Jim wrote in his journal,

> "This was a pleasant, restful, thrilling day. Flew in Jim Campbell's Seabee to Malibu Club in Canada. Spectacular place!"

The Princess Louisa Inlet is the most scintillating jewel in the crown of British Columbia inland waterways. Granite walls rise almost straight up from the water's edge to heights of five to eight-thousand feet. Over sixty crystal clear streams descend from the snow fields high above and cascade down the towering cliffs, ultimately joining the deep blue, mirror-smooth waters of the inlet. There, elegantly perched on primordial rock jutting into those cold waters, one-hundred miles north of Vancouver, exquisitely sits The Malibu Club! It is beyond the reach of ordinary transportation, lost in the pine forested mountains, and known chiefly to lumber men and wealthy West Coast yachters. It is a place of rapturous beauty.

When the Young Life staff first got wind that Jim was off in the wilds of Canada looking at a fourth campsite, their ability to think big was stretched to the breaking point. Even though some had vowed never to question him again, adding a resort in the Canadian wilderness was pushing things too far. And when the Young Life board first discovered that Jim was looking at property one couldn't even get to except by water, they emphatically told him, "Jim, boats are just not safe!" And in his characteristic manner he drawled, "Well, I'm sure glad the Alaska Steamship Company never heard of that!"

A year and a half after his first visit to Malibu, Jim met Tom Hamilton, the owner, to talk about a possible purchase. These were yet days when staff folks were lucky to find a dollar in their jeans. To consider purchasing a piece of property worth a million dollars seemed idiotic to most of them. This questioning and constant doubting was taking a toll on the 'Boss,' as Jim's staff affectionately called him. To step out in faith is a spiritual battle in and of itself, but when one's closest associates act as adversaries, it becomes an even lonelier road, void of affirmation and encouragement. From the realm of the senses, there was no way to acquire Malibu; it was simply beyond reach. Jim knew that. But Jim's battle was raging in the spiritual dimension, where faith is the key. It would have thrilled him if his staff would have joined him in the battle. Amazingly, Jim stayed focused on the spiritual realm, as these 1953 journal entries demonstrate:

> 11/3: *A wonderful conference with Tom Hamilton this afternoon. Am right in feeling like Malibu is about to be ours. I humbly thank God for all he is doing.*

> 11/4: *Had a fine conference with Tom Hamilton and Calder MacRay. Looks better all the time—I seem to have a sense of the Lord's sovereignty and omniscience in this. How little I have done. Nothing! But wonderful things continue to happen, things I believe God initiates. Great Kids rally in Pasadena—900 present.*

> 11/5: *Who knows—we may look back on this as a very historic day in Young Life. Tom Hamilton came while I was breakfasting with Jim McMikan. We quickly got into the Malibu deal and signed the agreement binding him to sell at the phenomenal price of $300,000, and binding me only to TRY. He is willing to take $150,000 , or less, down and make further concessions. How I do thank God. I've seldom felt so deeply grateful to Him. Great banquet tonight—300 or more present.*

Three days later, Jim, Add Sewell, Jim Campbell, and Bill Starr flew into Malibu for one final look at the property. Bill recalls, "The thought that overwhelmed my mind as we toured the place was that Jim spoke as if Malibu was ours, as though it was an accomplished fact . . . and I thought we were just flying up to look at it."

Jim's journal entry that night, November 8th, 1953:

> *To Malibu with Jim Campbell in Seabee. Add and Bill and I (again) completely bowled over with the possibilities it presents. Didn't even remember it was so beautiful and complete. Went to bed thanking and praising the Lord for His unfathomable goodness to us.*

Since Hamilton had asked for the deal to be consummated by the end of 1953, to allow him an income tax advantage, Jim saw that he had seven weeks to try for the money. He wasted no time. The rest of November and first three weeks of December found him in Seattle, Denver, Colorado Springs, Dallas, Memphis, Knoxville, Shelby, Cincinnati, Chicago, New York, Detroit, Minneapolis, St. Paul, Winnipeg, Vancouver, Tacoma, Portland, Berkeley, Redwood

(left) Jim, at the Malibu Club in British Columbia, Canada, 1955.

(below) Excited and awe-struck guests being welcomed at the Malibu Club, Jim's incredible resort for kids in the Canadian wilderness. Jim had this ship, the Malibu Princess, specially built to bring campers in and out of the very remote location.

City, Nashville, Los Angeles, and numerous points in between. It was a whirlwind travel schedule covering 23,000 miles, over twenty cities, and hundreds of contacts. It was also a period where Jim felt blessed by numerous 'miracles.' Finally, December 21st, he wrote in his journal:

> A most historic day! We went into escrow on the Malibu transaction this morning! Everybody very happy! The Lord has been wonderfully good in permitting us great forward strides.

To some it seemed that Jim had pulled another rabbit from his hat. Could he also walk on water, or maybe feed a whole camp on just one hamburger? For some of Jim's staff, admiration for the boss gave way to a type of adoration, and a dangerous die was cast. Human beings cannot afford to deify one another, for all people have human frailties.

Jim was not deceived about the source of his power:

"The best I know, I go where God leads, but oftentimes I do not know. I have to rely on the fact that He is great enough and good enough to guide me. And when He does guide me, He is also great enough to get me where He wants me. I am a feeble being. I don't know God's plans. It is sad to me when someone tries to figure out God's plan. I can think and earnestly pray, but in the final analysis I have to go back to this glorious, revealed fact: God is here! He is here to see me through and committed to seeing that I stay in His path. Paul said that God is able to make His grace abound towards us, that we will always have a sufficiency.

"God is able; I am unable. I'm a weakling. I'm blind. I can't figure out His way nor can I see ahead. But recognizing that we are not able to find God's way is probably the first reaction our hearts need in connection with the leadership of God's Spirit. He takes special care of weaklings! "My grace is sufficient for thee, for My strength is made perfect in weakness" [2 Cor. 12:9, KJV] He rejoices to move us along in His divine pattern when we come to Him, weak, hopeless, and helpless in ourselves. Go day by day, through every trying decision, with this great sovereignty of God in the forefront of your mind. I am God's. God will lead. He has given His Word. He will not let go of me.

"I am utterly disgusted with this tendency to worship human leaders. I wanted to swat a guy recently over some things he said concerning me. He missed the whole point by trying to pour a little anointing oil on Jim Rayburn. He gave the picture the wrong slant. If I have anything at all, I received it from God. If I differ in any positive way from others, it's only because God has touched me. We have no right to be bowing to anybody and saying, "Oh, isn't he wonderful." Who's wonderful? Jesus Christ is!

"My friend, if it so happens that one of God's servants has taken the gifts given him and has so lived out Christ that the glory of the Lord Jesus shows through the dull clay of that human vessel, then do you know who you ought to praise? Jesus Christ! Not the clay vessel. The vessel's just in the way. Jesus Christ just shows a little bit through the human clay of our lives. He doesn't really show in the fullness of His splendor. What a silly idea, bowing down and worshipping an old vessel of clay. That old cracked pot won't do any good. All right, then, let's not worship cracked pots. That'll make us all crackpots."

Compassion

CHRISTIANITY began in a great adventure. In those first days when the Master was presenting his way of living to men who had vision and courage enough to try it, discipleship was a costly spiritual exercise. The life to which Jesus summoned men required insight and bravery to undertake and fortitude to continue. Who, at first, could have dreamed that it ever would become in the eyes of multitudes a stiff and finished system to be passively received?

Faith, in the New Testament, was a matter of personal venturesomeness. It involved heeding and following that 'voice within.' It was not faith in formal creeds, for no creeds had yet been written; it was not faith in the New Testament, for the New Testament was not yet in existence; it was not faith in a certain theology, as that too was not a part of Christianity. It certainly wasn't faith in the church as we think of it today, as the institutional church didn't come into existence for hundreds of years following Christ's resurrection. In those days following the crucifixion of Jesus Christ, faith involved a vital and dynamic personal relationship with Christ through the indwelling Holy Spirit.

In the faith of the early church, this dynamic relationship with the living God within was the central reality. Faith was not a matter of thought or an issue of doctrines and dogmas. It sprang directly from vivid, commanding, indubitable, personal experience.

Today, so many are enslaved in a spiritless, counterfeit "Christianity," that people led of God's Spirit are frequently viewed as rebels, dreamers, or heretics.

Jim was burdened for those who didn't know of this spiritual realm. His experience of the Holy Spirit produced in him a compassion for young people that he earnestly wished to communicate to his staff. He later realized that some on his staff had never had a spiritual encounter. In a mid-fifties speech to his coworkers, he said, "I've enough people in this room to turn the world upside down for Jesus Christ, if all were true, born again Christians." In the following talk, he speaks about his own experience, and Jesus' compassionate treatment of people:

> Much to my surprise, I've found in going around the country that so many people on the staff of Young Life never had any kind of experience like I did, and for that matter didn't know about mine. And so it's been a while now that I've thought we should talk more about theology—the glorious truths concerning our faith. So far as I am concerned, personally, there would have been no Young Life at all without Dr. Lewis Chafer's course in soteriology.

> My whole life was completely changed when I found out the Holy Spirit was a real person—God, living in my life, doing things for me that I could never do myself. I read in God's word that men's eyes are to be filled with the person and the glory of the Lord Jesus Christ, and it is the Holy Spirit's business to make it so—only He can make it so. Bow down to the influences of the Spirit, bow down and open your heart to all His wonderful person and leadership, and your gaze will be concentrated on Jesus Christ.

> The greatest thing about the Lord Jesus Christ while He was on His way to the cross to die for our sins was His treatment of people—all kinds of folks. I am particularly interested in the phrase, "Jesus was moved with compassion." He saw a crowd of people and He was moved with compassion. He felt sorry for those people. His heart went out to them. Compassion is warmth, an entering in, a heartfelt desire to be on their side. Jesus saw the

multitude and they looked like scattered sheep—blundering, stumbling sheep. He had pity, He had love, He had warmth, but compassion is even more than that. He had sympathy for their plight, and sympathy for their viewpoint.

The Lord Jesus was never cross, He was never surprised by people's evil ways. Only two things ever surprised Jesus. A young fellow from a pagan country really trusted Him. He had a servant, desperately ill, and he came to Jesus and mentioned this fact. Jesus decided to go to his house, remember? The young officer of the Roman army said, "No, don't come down to my house," and he gave two of the most amazing reasons you ever heard. He said first of all, "I'm not even worthy that you should come under my roof," and second, "You don't need to. You can take care of the healing by remote control, You're in charge of life; you run the whole business." I don't know how that Roman officer knew that. I'm sure he didn't find it out in Rome. He was an officer in the occupying army, yet he knew it. And Jesus was astonished! He hadn't seen faith like that anywhere, even among His own people. On another occasion he was astonished that the people didn't believe. After all the works He did, after all the evidence was in, they still didn't believe. Remember that! Unbelief and belief are the two most astonishing things in the world.

I am committed to emulating Jesus Christ's example with regard to people. I want to have the same attitude toward people that Jesus had. This is my commitment, and this is my motivation. I want a heart like Jesus Christ's, and that's plainly known to be possible, even for sinners like me. God sends his Spirit to live in our hearts once we've truly believed in Jesus, for the plain and simple reason that we can't live up to His standards about love. But He can! And his Holy Spirit can make us that way too!

Jesus came down from a mountain and there was a great big crowd following Him, and a leper came to Him and worshipped Him. Lepers were absolutely vile. They had to stand outside the city and yell, "Unclean" " at the top of their lungs before they could even come into town, and they had to enter on the other side of the street. Nobody touched a leper. Mark's account says he knelt down before Jesus and cried, "Lord, if you wanted to, you could make me well." And Jesus reached out and touched him, the only person in the whole civilized world that would think of touching a leper.

Nobody is going to hurt in the presence of Jesus. He cared about people, people that didn't matter, people you usually don't care about. A little crook wanted to see Jesus, but he was too short. There was always too big a crowd around Him. So he ran down the Jerico road and climbed into a sycamore tree. Jesus passed under the tree and looked up and saw him. He didn't say, "You little crook, this mob behind me hates your insides. It would ruin my reputation if I associated with you. Take a good look, 'cause I'm going by." No! He said to the little crook, "Come on down, I'm going to go home with you." A little extortioner, despised by the self-righteous crowd that frequently pursued Jesus, was offered divine companionship in the presence of the whole bunch. Jesus never cared what somebody else thought. He loved people. That little guy, walking by the side of the Savior down to his house for supper, felt nine feet tall all the way home!

And there was another crook, remember? A crook that was fastened to a cross, a criminal, dying for his crime. His companion in crime was also on a cross. But on the center cross was One who was dying for people who have trouble with crime. His lifeblood was flowing down the old, rugged cross. And the crook turned and said, "Lord, remember me." He had no chance to go and make anything right. He had no chance to go and live an ethical, godly life, to prove that he meant business with Christ. Out of his misery and suffering and guilt he simply said, "Lord, remember me." And the dying Savior turned on his bloody cross and said to the crook, "You're going with me, today. We'll be together in Paradise." To a crook in a tree He offered friendship and compassion. To a crook on a cross He offered heaven. Jesus loved people.

Then there's that touching story of the woman He met at the well. She was a messed-up person if there ever was one. She had already divorced five husbands. It was probably a record for those days. He didn't talk to her about what a miserable sinner she *was. He talked to her about who God is. He didn't condemn her. He merely mentioned the fact that there were five preceding husbands, and that the present man wasn't really her husband. She went back to town and told the whole crowd, "Come on out and see this fellow who's been talking to me." She wouldn't have done that if He had whaled her over the head for being an adulteress. Compassion means gentleness and pity and sympathy and warmth. And Jesus Christ had compassion.*

Then in the eighth chapter of John, those self-righteous rascals, the Pharisees, dragged in a woman caught in the very act of adultery. And Jesus delivered her in a way that's become famous down through the ages. "The law says to stone her, so what do we do about that?" her accusers asked. Jesus' answer was, "The one who hasn't sinned, you throw the first rock." They slunk away. From the eldest to the youngest, they faded out of the picture. Then Jesus did a tender and touching thing, because he had compassion. He reached down and with His finger started making marks in the sand.

Did you ever stop and ask yourself why He did that? He had a pretty touchy situation on His hands. Why did He do that? Why, if you've been caught red-handed in some sin you don't want somebody standing you up eyeball to eyeball! It was a nice, gentle thing to do, to lean down and busy himself with His finger in the sand. He could treat her that way because He was going to die for her, and because He knew that His love would reach out and wrap itself around her heart, and she'd cling to Him forever. He was the ransom payment. Payment for sin was a serious, bloody, expensive business. God never treated sin lightly, but he never roughed up sinners.

Jesus made up a story one day. He had only two characters in this story, one a good man, the other a bad man. And He made the bad man a hero! The good man went up front in the church and prayed a long-winded prayer, a ridiculous kind of prayer when you really analyze it. But the bad man, he just barely plunked down into the back seat. He wasn't used to church, didn't even feel at home there. And he beat his chest and said, "God be merciful to me, a sinner." And the beautiful ending to

Jesus' story is that the bad man went home all right; the poor "good" fellow was still in a box.

Jesus came to seek and to save people who are lost. So if we are going about His business in the New Testament way, then we've got to be very understanding, and very loving about people that are off the track. He was, and we've got to be.

I am identified with the modern institutional church. I am a member of one of the most institutional of them all, a Presbyterian minister in good standing in my presbytery for twenty-one years. Quite a record for a fellow in my line of work. The Presbyterians frown on anything they can't control, and I'll give you a clue—they can't control me. I am identified, and I trust loyally so and constructively so, with the local, organized church. But I am also engaged in the sincere attempt to get back to what New Testament Christianity was really all about. The heart and center of it was Jesus Christ and people.

I want a chance to tell all the young people growing up in our nation about Jesus Christ and His love for them. I want to tell them in terms they can understand and appreciate. I want to tell them with their hearts and lives wide open so I know they're listening. So I simply have to emulate the example of Paul, the greatest Christian missionary, who said to be all things to all people, doing everything possible to be like they want me to be. It's a wonderful thing to have kids come every week after camp and say, "Jim, I never heard this before, or else I wasn't listening before." We take them up Chimney Rock and scare them, and we take them up the snow slides and get them frozen; we ramble around, we feed them too much, we go all out all the time to win their confidence and friendship. It's no wonder that they say, "I never heard it before." Nobody ever took many pains to see that they listened before! I'll do everything to see that kids are listening.

I know so-called Christian people that the other people in town just want to spit on. These folks have never gone an inch out of their way for anyone. They don't care about people. They're preaching Christ all right, but there's something missing! I'm afraid, if the truth were known, that most "Christians" are like that—they never closed in with the Savior, they never were touched by the Spirit, they never got the gospel, they never really opened the door of their hearts—'cause when Jesus comes into a life, He makes a difference.

Hudson Taylor went to inland China. He had a burden like the burden that Paul the apostle had. He was determined that those people farthest out were going to hear about Jesus Christ. H. Taylor grew long hair and wore Chinese clothes—that must have been awfully hard for an Englishman to do. You know how stuck the English people are; to do anything that hasn't been done for the last 976 years would be a real trial. But he did it for Jesus' sake, and probably H. Taylor and those that followed him reached more people for Jesus Christ than anyone in modern history. Probably the church is standing strong and true today in the midst of that Communist culture because of Hudson Taylor and those that followed him.

Adoniram Judson went to Burma with his heart aflame for Jesus Christ. He was determined he was going to reach those people for the Savior. For seven long years he lived with those Burmese people and he never got a convert—not one. You read the story of how they treated him, you read of the terrible way he suffered, you read of the way his wife died, and you'll think impossible, foolish, ridiculous, the mission board back home pestering him all the time to get some results, to please put some numbers on his reports. But he kept on living for and loving Burmese people. Finally at the end of seven years he had a convert—a little girl accepted Jesus Christ as her Savior, the first Christian in Burma. The church grew strong and true, because A. Judson loved Jesus Christ and meant business about following Jesus' example.

The great Robert Moffat, father-in-law of David Livingstone, went to the Cameroons in the early days of African missions, even before Livingstone had opened up the dark continent. There in the Cameroons was a wild and vicious tribe headed by the chief, Africaner, a murderer, a brutal, sadistic savage. Moffat set his heart to reach those people, and he started with the worst one, the poorest prospect, Africaner. For years he befriended Africaner, for years he protected him from the British govern-

ment, his own government. Moffat befriended Africaner, who became the first convert of his tribe.

So the story goes, down through Christian history. Our young people today, six or eight-million in the high-school age alone, are waiting, waiting for somebody to care about them like that. I mean there are six or eight-million in our nation that nobody has ever talked to about Jesus Christ, that nobody has ever said a prayer for, that nobody has ever cared about. There are millions of them in our own nation, and they are waiting for somebody to care about them enough to take the time and trouble to pour out compassion on them, to prove their friendship, to bridge this tragic and terrible gap that exists in our culture between teenagers and adults—to emulate the example of Jesus Christ. They're waiting for somebody, and I believe you and I and the people whose lives we touch have to be that somebody. I pray that we'll lift up our eyes to the multitudes, like Jesus did, 'cause a million kids is a multitude, two-million is a whale of a multitude, and six or eight-million I can't even imagine.

It is the Divine Spirit that implants such burdens into the hearts of Christ's people. Jim had awakened late to the realization that some of his people were not so "fired up," not so burdened for the task at hand as he was. He figured that theological studies might provide his staff with that same 'fire.' After all, learning theology from Dr. Chafer had largely been his route to a deeper understanding and experience of the Holy Spirit. Jim wasn't willing, however, to lose his coworker's services for several years while they studied at a seminary. As he saw it, there was only one solution—to start his own graduate school.

The first class of seven students traveled to their professors, recapturing a medieval touch. From September 1951 to June 1952, the "station wagon grad school" was on the road, visiting professors from Los Angeles to Seattle to New York. In 1954 the Young Life Institute began as a summer school at Star Ranch with twenty-five students.

Brad Curl, a former member of Jim's staff, talks about the kind of faith Jim hoped to develop in his leaders:

"Jim was calling sharp young men and women to sacrifice, to risk starving to death for the purpose of reaching kids. At times, when the testing came, there wasn't any food in the cupboards. Jim was pushing his people toward the spiritual peaks, asking them to place all their needs in the hands of God. For his staff there was always the temptation to think, 'Man, there are folks out there no smarter than me, same education as I have, and they're making five times what I'm making.' Jim was calling his people to be suffering servants, to take up the cross. He knew there wasn't any other way to get the job done. He had a burden from the Spirit, and he wanted his people to feel it too.

"What we largely have today is a crossless faith. Many people don't want to pay the price anymore. The irony is that the sharpest young men and women, tomorrow's generation of leaders, are looking for the kind of risk-it-all commitment that Jim called his people to in the first place."

Breakdown

CHAPTER *13*

GOD'S adversary had thrown everything imaginable at Jim and Maxine from the moment of Jim's spiritual breakthrough: nervous breakdowns, a ruptured appendix, attacks by the institutional churches, lightning bolts, forest fires, increased migraine attacks, financial stress, drug problems and marital discord. Throughout the fifties, these battles raged on.

Maxine had vein surgery on her legs in 1949. A hysterectomy in 1950 brought on surgical menopause. She was back in the hospital in 1952 for another leg operation. That same year saw dental surgery. In 1954, a complicated medical procedure was performed on her feet. Two years later, it was spinal surgery, another attempt to correct her injured disk. Beginning in 1952, she fought her own battle with migraine headaches. Discouraged by Jim's and her own failing health, Max lost the battle to control her weight. By the mid-fifties she had ballooned to over two-hundred pounds. Thereafter, it was difficult to get her out of the house; feeling that she was unattractive, she lost all interest in socializing with others.

By 1954 Jim was physically and emotionally spent. Migraine headaches were occurring more frequently, and sleepless nights were commonplace. Excerpts from his daily journal:

1/4/1954: *During this whole week my work at the office almost unbearably tough for me—Maxine sick all week. No encouragement from any quarter—no money for back salaries—For me, at least, this must be a terrific time of testing.*

And, on February 28, he wrote, *Good time of prayer this a.m.—and enjoyed studying Romans in "Phillips" this afternoon. Very concerned that I am not doing my best for the Lord—also can't find out why I am at such a very low ebb physically.*

On March 2, *A rather poor day—I am just "low" every way—especially in production.*

"Jim was totally exhausted and sinking fast," Maxine recalled, "I knew he needed help. I wasn't in any position to assist him as I was having such a struggle in my own right, but I could see he was in trouble; someone had to come to his aid. I contacted some friends who gave the money for Jim to take a trip around the world. He left in October and was gone for three months."

Jim desperately needed this reprieve. There were several areas of intense stress in his life. In a relatively short span, his Texas experiment had mushroomed into a sizable outreach. Jim had unintentionally created, and found himself the pastor of, a church. It was not a typical, organized, denominational church, but a twentieth-century Christian church searching for its heritage in the pages of the New Testament. It was an orphan church, a motherless child, thrown into the open field (Ezek. 16:4-5). There were no buildings, no organ, no confessional, and precious little structure. What was called Young Life was simply a diverse, lovable group of people united under Jim's leadership by a sincere concern for kids and varying commitments to Christ. Providing direction for this unlikely group had become a full-time job.

All the duties usually incumbent on a corporate president were Jim's, and these responsibilities alone were another full-time situation. This was the hat in Jim's closet that didn't fit very well, the one that gave him headaches, but it was the hat his board of directors most wanted him to wear. They could relate to that hat; they were familiar with it—many of them were corporate presidents as

132

well. As with any corporate board of directors, their main concern was financial stability. Was the ship on sound financial waters or not?

There was no way Jim could guarantee smooth sailing over calm financial seas. The challenge facing a disciple is to walk with Christ on top of the waves, to exercise faith, to believe in and trust the prompting of the Spirit within. When Peter stopped to look at the waves on which he was standing he started to sink. Likewise, when a disciple of Christ starts to count his money, he will sink as well. Jim had learned that when his eyes were stayed on Jesus Christ, he didn't sink. The worst thing he could do was to count his money; it took his eyes off the Lord.

But Jim was not a superman. The financial needs of his people and the monetary concerns of his board rose like giant waves of pressure threatening to engulf him. Further, it drained him to be constantly doubted by his close associates. The contention surrounding him was drowning the quiet whisper of God's Spirit. The pressure was unreal, and it was utterly destroying his health.

The world cruise that Max arranged was a godsend. By trip's end the interval between migraines had jumped to three weeks; Jim was feeling like a new man. But the pressures he had left in San Francisco were there to greet him when he docked in New York. Excerpts from his 1955 journal show the sudden change in mood as he terminated the European portion of his venture, boarded the Queen Mary in Southampton, and sailed for New York:

12/26/1954: *Talked to Maxine this a.m. Had a very good morning just praying and reading the Word. Skied this afternoon. Powder to my hips at times. I didn't fall once. Must be getting better.*

12/30: *A wonderful day! Rod and I took the train to the Gornergrat this a.m. and skied back to town—about ten miles! From 11,300 feet to 5,000 feet. What a sport! The greatest ski runs I ever saw—even better than yesterday—and faster. Spent the afternoon in prayer and fellowship with Rod.*

1/2/1955: *Read the Word several hours today.*

1/5: *Wonderful time in prayer. Word precious.*

1/9: *The improvement in my devotional life the last few weeks very real and important to me.*

1/18: *Leaving London for Southampton and Queen Mary.*

Jim, amid mountains that matched his vision, skiing the Swiss Alps in 1954.

1/21: *Studied the Word and prayed this whole day through. A great day!*

1/22: *One of the greatest days in prayer and the Word.*

1/23: *Another grand day of worship and prayer.*

1/24: *Arrived in New York at 10 a.m. Norm and Eastern staff met me. A hard, lonesome day.*

1/25: *To Chicago for board of directors meeting tomorrow. Migraine—first one of the year.*

1/26: *Board meeting in Chicago. Wish I hadn't come. Could just as well have gone home for all the good it did. Very disappointed—prone to be discouraged about the condition of the work. But that means the Lord must take a larger place with me. His will is ALL that matters.*

Administrative details, management hassles, fund-raising duties, board meetings, committee meetings, and demanding schedules all triggered long runs of vicious migraines. As God does not call people to self-destruction, it is difficult to imagine that these activities were a necessary part of Jim's calling.

In 1956 a medical doctor from Washington state prescribed for Jim a new wonder drug named Dexamyl. It was almost guaranteed to energize him, improve his overall health, and possibly help the headache situation. Jim's initial prescription was for one-thousand capsules! Almost instantly, the new drug had a marvelous effect; Jim's health and energy level soared to new heights and remained there for several years.

Jim had given little emphasis to job descriptions, personnel files, organizational charts, policy formulation, and so on. As his outfit continued to grow, however, his lack of interest in administrative details mushroomed into a sizable problem. Jim's board, deeply concerned by the situation, adopted an "Organizational Plan" in January, 1957. Under the guise of relieving Jim of administrative concerns, this plan specified new lines of authority, a new organizational structure, specific job descriptions, and "effective programs of financial planning and budgetary control."

This new plan, however well intentioned, was the genesis of a tragedy, as it called for Jim's staff to become heavily involved in administration and management. Jim wished his staff to be freed from these distractions. One of the biggest differences between the Young Life work of Jim's day, and the Young Life work of today, is right here, on this very issue of the job description of an area director.

Young Life, as a whole, would be immensely blessed by returning to Jim's viewpoint on this matter. Far too much of a staff person's time is taken up with paperwork, and administrative details. Jim would never have approved such an arrangement. As he viewed it:

> God has given us a great and holy task. I cannot think of any area of the church's activity more critical than the one we (Young Life leaders) face everyday. We desperately need adult committee people, people who are wise and full of God's Spirit, to handle the business end of things, to build the platform of support upon which the Young Life leader stands. But here is where we have to stand—we will give ourselves continually to prayer, and to sharing Christ with the high school crowd. And that's all! Committee people must do their task so that we may do ours. That's where we HAVE TO STAND—given ONLY to the ministry of God's Word, and prayer.

By the early sixties Jim was beginning to experience adverse reactions to the new "wonder drug" that he'd been taking for the last four years: severe stomach disorders, mild tremors, irritability, and severe insomnia, causing intense fatigue. All are symptoms of drug poisoning. Tragically, his doctors continued to supply him with these questionable medications. The long-range effects would be devastating.

Dexamyl, an amphetamine known several decades later as a type of "speed," causes marked insomnia, irritability, hyperactivity, and personality changes. Dizziness, tremors, headaches, dryness of the mouth, diarrhea, and various gastrointestinal disturbances are other adverse reactions. At one time or another, Jim experienced every one of these symptoms, yet no one suspected the cause, least of all his doctors.

Eventually stomach ulcers led to surgery in June of 1961. This was the coup de grace to Jim's elusive search for good health. In an operation no longer performed just a few years later, the nerve controlling the flow of digestive juices to the stomach was severed, and over half of his stomach removed. It was a rare day thereafter when his digestive system functioned at all.

The downhill course of Jim's health runs in strange contrast to the ever blossoming longings of his heart. And his commitment to his Lord seemed almost hard to believe. Take, for example, the time he called his staff men together for three days of prayer at Frontier Ranch. His journals:

9/11/1961: 45 to 50 staff men began our three day session of prayer this a.m. There was considerable blessing—difficult to evaluate—and a surprising amount of time spent in actual prayer. Good attention.

9/12: An AMAZING DAY. Up at 4:55 a.m. All the group praying together at 5:30 a.m. First half hour praise and thanks— then I was impelled to speak to them of our mission and the great things—admonishing it was time to think positively—not always "what is wrong." Amazing, unexpected response and an "inspired" time of prayer before breakfast. The rest of the day was outstanding—it is hard to know what to say about a time like this.

Day three went the same as day two, and this special meeting was closed with Jim leading a communion service. Then, next day, Jim drove to Colorado Springs with five staff men joining him in his car. He wrote in his diary that they had enjoyed some good time of prayer en route. Yet, not many days later:

10/4/1961: Will I ever understand why it is often so hard to get down to business and pray—specially when I have so very much for which to be thankful? Prayer with the office crew. Letters to board and staff notifying them of the marvelous wind up of our

137

fiscal year. Home to look at World Series—N.Y. 2, Cincy 0. To office—fast work on a lot of letters. To "Eagle" (train) at 5:55 p.m. Dinner—and an excellent time of prayer.

Several weeks later, Jim picked up his new convertible in Detroit and drove it home to Colorado. This too served as an opportunity to commune with his creator while he drove cross country:

11/22/1961: *A most unusual day. Length of time engaged in prayer itself unusual—unparalleled perhaps. The degree of concentration throughout much of the day was seemingly higher than any I've achieved. A third amazing fact was the enormous range of subjects and people. Then, fourth, was the definite subject matter of the prayers, including specific requests for individuals—and the amazing number of matters that the Spirit brought to my attention for prayer. Lunch just across the Kansas border. Got sleepy about 3 p.m. so stopped at a very nice place one mile west of Belleville. Nap—read—dinner—T.V.*

Little did Jim know or even suspect what a barbaric surgical procedure had been performed upon him that June day in 1961. Not many years later medical science had a non-surgical cure for a stomach ulcer, but for Jim the cure came late. This primitive surgery would play into the hands of that unseen enemy that had chased after Jim ever since his wedding day.

Visions
And Controversy
CHAPTER *14*

WITH increased international exposure from the mid-fifties through the early sixties, Jim's burden for kids had become global. Although he visited some of the worst ghettos known, he frequently rubbed shoulders with rich and politically powerful people as well. Whether he was sleeping in a mud hut in Africa or a palace in Europe, Jim's warmth, personality, and savoir-faire made him equally at home with people of high station and of low.

Jim had a sensitivity to other cultures that would put many diplomats to shame. Long before terms such as *global community* became fashionable, he viewed the world as a global village. He had seen life as it is experienced by the poorest of the poor—in Pakistan, India, Africa, the American Indian reservations, and the hinterlands of South America. There were few places Jim hadn't been and very few people he didn't love. Indeed, his heart was filled with the Divine Spirit that looks upon the multitude and feels compassion.

In a world that prefers black-robed and white-collared clergy, Jim was far too cosmopolitan for some people's tastes. He not only knew which wine he preferred, he knew the vintage. In the company of intellectuals preferring conversation about Plato, Socrates, Kant, or Hegel, Jim was always well versed and eager for conversation. I vividly remember his saying in that deep, slow, Jimmy Stewart

139

Jim on a Navajo Reservation in the four-corners area, 1950. He had been permitted to view a sacred ceremony performed by the medicine man, to heal a sick baby.

drawl, "Why, those European kids always want to talk to me about existentialism; these kids here in the United States don't even know what the word means. All they want to talk about is last year's football team, who's taking who to the prom, or this year's cheerleading squad. Why, it makes one wonder what's wrong with our educational system."

For all his depth, Jim's ever-present sense of humor would bubble to the surface on any occasion. In reporting on a trip abroad to a rather large and conservative church, Jim injected, "Why, the carpets on that ship were so plush, I ran around all day without my pants on, and nobody knew the difference." In a chapel message to his younger staff trainees Jim came forth with this jewel, "It is impossible for us to please all the people in the organized church. There are fundamentalists who say I am too liberal, there are liberals who

140

say I am too fundamental, and there are conservatives who say I am too radical. Fundamentally, I am a liberal conservative."

In the spring of 1959, Jim had his first exposure to East Berlin. It was an experience that changed his life. Horrified by what he'd seen and experienced of life under Communist rule, Jim determined to fight back. Wasting no time, he took eleven of his men to Europe in November, 1959. For most, it was their first exposure to foreign shores. Jim felt like a father taking his boys out to dine at their first gourmet restaurant. Journal excerpts tell the story:

11/13: *A restful day. The food is wonderful, and the sea is unbelievably calm. I think my boys are getting a big kick out of it. The ship and service are perfect in every way. The boys sure looked swell "dressed" for dinner.*

11/24: *To East Berlin with the whole crowd this afternoon. A powerful experience. I'll never forget the nineteen-year-old's moving prayer, "We'll never again see each other here . . . only in the kingdom."*

11/24: *Where but in Berlin could one have such a heart searching experience? We went to the Marienfelds Reception Center this morning. Sat in on a "trial" of a young East German who has tried for two years to reach his wife in the West—has given up everything. Some wonderful time with dozens of little kindergarten kids—they call me "Uncle Jim." Interviewed a nineteen-year-old girl who just escaped from Leipzig. Great to be with Bill, Tim, and Orien.*

11/25: *An hour with Mayor Willy Brandt this morning. Also had a great experience in a teenage boys' camp—about two-hundred boys who'd escaped to the West after their parents "mysteriously disappeared." Grand and shocking case histories by personal account.*

It frightened Jim to see the complacency in his own country towards this demonic Soviet empire. Outside of the military, he found most Americans rather apathetic towards those suffering under Communist regimes. It seemed to him that most Communist revolutionaries were more dedicated to world change than Christians seemed to be. By exposing his men to the horrors of Soviet Communism, Jim hoped to raise the level of their concern. He told many a high school assembly, and a myriad of churches, about his discoveries in East Germany:

Jim with his dear friend, Dr. Hilde Reinartz, laying a wreath where Olga Segler lost her life in a desperate jump for freedom, attempting to escape East Berlin.

142

People tell me, "That's all right, Jim; they're over there and we're over here. It's not our problem." But anybody who says that is not only a traitor to a free way of life, he's a traitor to the human race.

West Berlin was a little island of freedom in a sea of slavery. To walk from freedom into horror, you only had to cross the street. With my heart in my mouth, I took my daughter's hand and walked across that line. I wondered if we'd ever get back. We hadn't walked ten feet before we felt the difference. Not a single person smiled; we could smell the fear in the people. Not one single person on the streets dared to greet us. Fear permeated the atmosphere.

We met East Berlin University kids, and lots of high school kids, and they all told us the same thing, "We can't go where we want to; we can't say what we want to; we can't get together in groups; we can't go to church; we can't study what we want to."

I thought, "Surely this can't be true in the world we live in today, and it surely can't be true that people will sit idly by and not do anything for all the folks who are suffering under this dehumanizing system of government."

Jim's convictions ran deep. The weight of suffering humanity was tearing at his heart. He was a man with a burden, a heavenly compassion implanted within by the Spirit of God. There was no escaping the heart-wrenching memory of smileless faces and empty eyes behind the Iron Curtain. Nor could Jim turn his back on the desperate need of the world's teenagers, so many of whom do not have an adult friend who truly cares about them.

These deep concerns gave birth to another miracle. He had dreamed for years of building a lodge for adults, a glorified Lookout, from which he could share his work and the burdens of his heart with a large number of guests at one time.

I first became aware of Jim's plan while hiking with him on the slopes of Mt. Harvard, just outside Buena Vista, Colorado. As we sat to rest on a large boulder, high atop a gorgeous ridge, he told me of his dream. Right where we were sitting he wanted to build his fantasy facility, a first-class resort to rival any hotel in the country.

And from that place he planned to share his work, his God, and his burdens with as many people as were led to him.

It was a glorious dream, but once again, most of his people had little enthusiasm for such an idea. The problem, as viewed by many on Jim's staff and several of his board of directors, was finding the money to pay for such a project. Curiously, Jim's track record of acquiring every other property never seemed to enter the minds of those who questioned him.

Jim's board of directors was an unusually affluent group; most were high-powered, monied businessmen. By and large, these men were not used to being followers or taking orders; in the business world, their word was law. In Young Life, however, Jim's word was law, and several on the board of directors at times resented his strong leadership style. Jim was rapidly becoming the number-one target in a deadly serious power struggle, and he had no idea.

A board member recalls: "When Jim would give his director's report we would sit there awestruck by the quality and imagination of the man. He was phenomenal! But as we got into the fiscal responsibility, or a judgment decision on economics, we were just torn apart as businessmen. There was such a gap between following Jim's leadership on the one hand and handling the economics to keep up with him on the other."

One of Jim's former staff analyzes the problem, "It's very unsettling for people who are close to someone like Jim—you know, a man who will grab his buddies an go sit on a mountain top to pray all night! It would have been easier on Jim if he'd been surrounded by more people who understood him, but that's not the point. One who's anointed can't afford to dwell upon that.

"There were fine people around Jim who were deeply challenged, if not upset, by his abandon to the great spiritual heights. They wanted to go along with him, but were struggling with the cost of doing so. People don't go easily into that ecstatic, joyous, costly, cross-bearing experience—they kick and scream a lot along the way. Whenever someone reaches for the heights like Jim did, he becomes such a threat! Usually, such a person has to pay the price for that; Jim certainly did."

Jim was a threat to a wider group than just his board of directors. Ever since he'd started his work with America's teenagers he had been roughed up by many of the mainline churches, many of which did not consider him a bona fide man of God because his work was done outside of their jurisdiction. Further, there can be no question that plain and simple jealousy was involved as well. Jim's work with teenagers was hugely successful and few mainline churches could say the same. Accordingly, there were few churches that were overjoyed with his success.

In a 1958 message to his staff, Jim commented, "We are all convinced Christians, and we believe in the church and we are engaged in church work. We believe that everyone who is a true believer in the Lord Jesus Christ is a member of His great church, and we further believe in the organized church." (Note that Jim made a distinction here between the Lord's great church, and the organized church.) "But I am sure you could say with me you don't know exactly what the organized church ought to be since it doesn't seem like it ought to be the way it is. I am quite sure that two-hundred-fifty different denominations in the United States alone doesn't look good in heaven. For sure it doesn't look or sound like the New Testament Church. I cannot imagine the Apostle Paul in Corinth coming and trying to feel out which denomination he was going to. But, happily, I have not the slightest notion how to fix it up if it were delivered to me. I am not a reformer." Then, tongue in cheek, Jim ended with, "The only thing I know to do would be for everybody to stop their foolishness and be Presbyterians."

This, of course, was said in jest, but it was not representative of Jim's true feelings on the subject. By the early sixties, many were the weeks that Jim would say to me, returning from Sunday church services (Presbyterian at that), "JimBo, I'm sorry church is so distasteful, so regimented, so boring. I don't want you to think that it represents Jesus Christ in any way. It doesn't represent Christ, it doesn't represent true Christianity, and it doesn't represent heaven. I hope you won't ever think it does."

I never said to Jim, "If it doesn't represent Christ, then why are we going to church every week?" Even though a very young man, I could sense his dilemma. Growing up, Jim wouldn't dare consider missing church—that would have been unthinkable. He was trying to dance to a new music of liberty, but the bondage of his boyhood religious indoctrination had his feet nailed to the floor. He wanted to set me free, but he couldn't quite feel comfortable in doing that. So, we went to church together, and he'd apologize all the way home. But to tell me that it didn't represent Christ, heaven, or true Christianity was something I never thought I'd hear him admit.

What a statement for a man to make who had probably led more young people to an encounter with the Lord Jesus Christ than almost anyone we can think of. But Jim didn't make this comment flippantly. It had taken him years to come to this conclusion. As stated in chapter one, Jim's family attended church whenever the doors were open; as a boy his life revolved around the local denomination.

As an adult, Jim had been one of the most popular Sunday school teachers his church in Colorado Springs had ever had. He had taken a class with only a handful of married couples and grown it to several-hundred. Jim had supported the organized church in every way he knew, but as his spiritual sensitivities matured he simply couldn't do so any longer. He felt it was up to the few true Christians in each church to bring the change. He'd say, "In a great big church of several-thousand members there ought to be at least ten to fifteen people there who really know and love the Savior. It is up to them to make their church in some way relevant to outsiders."

It had taken Jim many years to accept that, overall, the organized church was more a problem to Christianity than a part of it. Having made that determination, he became increasingly outspoken regarding the chasm between the New Testament ecclesia (the early family or body of believers) and the present day mainline churches. He could see little or no relationship.

Jim was growing, spiritually, and much of what he was coming to grips with wasn't easy for him. After all, he himself was an ordained Presbyterian minister in good standing within the denomination. But if truth be told, on returning from a Presbytery meeting he would usually comment, "This has been the longest, most boring, and most useless day of my life." How he loathed those meetings!

146

As far back as the early forties, Jim was frustrated with the organized church, as is seen in his diary entry of 10/25/1942:

A Real Red Letter Day—I spoke on John 4:14, 4:35, Proverbs 29:18. The churches lack of vision, apathy, complacence. The opportunities unheeded—all around us . . .

Jim was coming to realize that the Christian faith was the first, and only, belief in God ever to exist in human history that had no special buildings, no clergy, no special costumes, no special vocabulary, and no rituals. As Gene Edwards points out in his numerous books, the ecclesia was born in informality—the only templeless, clergyless, ritu‑alless religion in all of recorded history. What a distinction! And what a glory to the Savior who gave us the way to the Father! A way void of religion and religious practices.

Think of that. There was no church building, no education department, no membership committee, no visitation committee, no Sunday school, no mortgage, and no finance committee. There were no sermons, no ministers, no pews, no sacred desks (pulpits), and no one with his shirt on backwards. There was no missions committee, no women's mission society, no budget, no political involvement committee, not even a theology class. Best of all, perhaps, there was no ritualistic, structured 'service' to sit through. Today, we not only have a preprogrammed, structured hour to endure, it comes complete with a written schedule of the ensuing rituals. What all of this has to do with Jesus Christ is a mystery. If one can truly worship God in such an environment, wonderful, but most can't, and don't.

Jim had finally realized that when the early church got together, these were happy, joyous, family style get-togethers, meals, and celebrations. Members were brothers and sisters by a spiritual rebirth, sharing a wondrous mystery. Gatherings were held in private homes till the groups got too large and more homes were opened. Further, there was no ritualistic hour to meet, such as Sunday morning at 10:55 o'clock. The faith was spontaneous and exciting. There was nothing dull, boring, religious, or ritualistic about it.

Private homes were filled with folks who were experiencing a revelation of a risen, ascended, enthroned, and exalted Lord. The people were wild with joy, set free from the religious bondage of their past, and relished sharing with others what Jesus Christ meant to them. They had stepped from religious bondage into the light of liberty.

It didn't take long for all manner of human problems and human weaknesses to foul the waters, and things weren't perfect by any means. But there was notably less structure, ritual, and religion than is experienced today, and an infinitely higher awareness of God's indwelling Spirit.

These folks couldn't keep from sharing about this Lord who lived within them. Almost everyone had something to give to the group, and they did not look to a professional to fill up their empty buckets. It is safe to say that for the most part, their 'buckets' were full, full of the richness of a deep and liberating walk with their Lord.

As Jim entered his fifties he came to accept that this was not true of the organized church at all, and he said so, more emphatically with each year that passed. He was walking on a tightrope here, however, as many dear and personal friends of his were ministers of large denominational churches. Jim was a gentleman's gentleman, and had no wish to offend his colleagues, but he was increasingly concerned that thousands of young people who were new to the faith, overflowing with excitement and joy, had nowhere to go to experience the faith in a New Testament way. To plug those kids into a stiff religious system was to slowly snuff out the excitement and joy of walking with the Lord Jesus Christ. Jesus cannot be found in dry and boring religious environments. More often than not, joining the mainline religious establishment is the kiss of death to any excitement a new believer may be experiencing.

Back when Jim was pioneering his work with teenagers, he never thought twice about reforming the church. That was not his call or interest. He was simply so excited about his Lord and his growing work, that as he plowed ahead, he unintentionally created kind of a New Testament church. He didn't even realize he was doing it. He said it embarrassed him to be introduced as the founder of Young Life, because he never knew he was founding anything. But there are interesting similarities in Jim's early work to the New

Testament ecclesia. Sadly, as Jim's feelings about the organized church evolved, a few on his staff and board no longer found themselves in step. Division had finally come to Young Life, as it always seems to do wherever God is doing a great work.

History has proven that the more in touch a man or woman is with the Spirit of God, the less understood he or she will be by associates. Just look at the disciple's inability, time and again, to understand what Jesus was trying to teach them. There was nothing Jim could do to avoid being controversial; firstly, he was a visionary, secondly, he had a deep and sincere faith seldom understood by others, and thirdly, he was outspoken regarding his beliefs.

As the tumultuous sixties moved on, Jim found himself embroiled in controversy. He was pushing a most unpopular adult lodge project that his staff had little vision for and most on his board of directors did not want, he was nearly alone in his commitment to the international expansion of his work, and he was speaking out ever more candidly regarding the organized church, as in this message to his staff:

Jim, as he appeared about the time he was engulfed in controversy over the church, international expansion, and other projects—1962 to 1963. Those in his immediate family would recognize a migraine developing when this picture was taken. He had a telltale look about him.

Three years ago Bishop Russell Hubbard asked me what I'd do with the incredible problem in the organized church—to make the church be in touch with the secular community. Well, I was in the company of a dear friend, so I felt the freedom to speak my mind.

149

I told the bishop that I'd like to scrap about everything the church does, that we'd have to stop doing what we're doing and start over! I'd certainly scuttle the Sunday-school programs, in their present form, because kids over twelve years of age hate it. One can't teach about Christ in an environment that people hate. My idea is that Sunday school will have to be neither Sunday, nor school.

Kids can't wait until Friday afternoon when they can bust out of school for the weekend! So what do we Christians do? We insist they go back to school on Sunday morning! Of all the silly notions I have heard, that one tops the list!

I have some wonderful ideas concerning what you could do with a morning worship service. I believe there are forty-eight known ways, and forty-eight-thousand unknown ways, to have a time that would be creative, attractive, and help people's hearts flow out to God, which is just what worship is supposed to do. True worship almost never happens in church. You go to church to worship but in your innermost heart you know you haven't. Why, there's been almost no creative effort in worship service since the Vikings discovered Labrador.

There's no evidence in the Bible that any New Testament church acted remotely like we act! I can't understand such foolishness! One of the things that gripes me is that a third of many services is taken to announce the extra-curricular activities. I wonder how much time the Apostle Paul spent telling about the men's club Friday evening fish fry? For goodness sake, where did we get so far off the ball? We act like we don't even know what Jesus Christ, the gospel, the Christian life, and worship is about.

I go to church, sit through the whole dull business, and go on home figuring I'll bore myself silly for an hour the next Sunday repeating the whole ritual. Pastors have told me that they know this isn't right, but they don't know what to do about it. Just recently, a pastor of one of the largest churches in the country told me, with tears in his eyes, that he was uncertain if there was one true Christian in his congregation. And he has four-thousand members!

The institutional church has brought us such a messed-up type of Christianity there's no justification in even calling it by that name. When will the church start doing true church work, and stop considering ushering, and passing the collection plate, church work? If there's anything that's truly ridiculous, it's what we call church work! You can be the most active guy in church, and make a list of all the things you do: count the money, participate in clean-up day, usher, sponsor the youth group, an so on, but by the standards of the New Testament, not one thing on your list is church work. Not a thing! Church work is done out in society.

Christ is the strongest, grandest, most attractive personality ever to grace the earth. But a careless messenger with the wrong approach can reduce all this magnificence to the level of boredom . . . It is a crime to bore anyone with the Gospel!

Some of Jim's close friends in the institutional churches understood what he was saying and agreed with him. But they were men and women who were learning from Jim, and they had open minds and 'eyes to see,' as Christ calls it. There were other people in Jim's orbit, a few on his staff and board, who took offense at such a strong negative stance toward organized religion. After all, Jim had once seemed to be a staunch ally of the organized church, and now? Further, such strong, straight-forward talk might influence the donations as well. This, no doubt, was a huge concern to a staff and board who had wrestled with monetary uncertainty since the earliest days, and who were constantly seeking more financial security.

Jim had the leadership abilities, anointing, intelligence, and warmth to handle being controversial. He'd been that since he'd started his work. What was rapidly changing in his situation was the devastating decline in his personal health, which opened the door to those few who disagreed with him to stir up the waters of division. His situation was increasingly precarious. Jim continued on, oblivious of gathering storm clouds on his horizon.

Exile

THE majority of Jim's staff respected him greatly, even though they questioned him at times. Some, unfortunately, may have idolized him. Four who worked with him recall their impressions:

"I was on Jim's staff in the early fifties. I didn't know him well, as I was young and somewhat intimidated by such a great man. I'd heard a lot of people pray, but when I heard Jim pray . . . I was awed; when I'd hear him talk to God, I felt that I was standing before God too."

"I've never met a person with so much charisma. He reminded me very much of Will Rogers. His effect on people was powerful, which gave him an influence I'm not sure he fully grasped. And that frightened me some. Had the human side of Jim taken over, he could have led us anywhere. He was an amazing man; I think most of us would have followed him to the edge of hell."

"As a speaker, he was the best I ever heard. I'd laugh so hard I'd feel drained, and then I'd weep as Jim took us to the feet of Jesus Christ. He could have led us in so many directions, but he always took us to Jesus Christ. Many of us, however, were following Jim, and he was following Christ. We didn't have that same intimacy with God that he knew."

"Jim was a man's man, a man with courage, a man with guts, a man who'd lay his life on the line for what he believed. I've never met a person with so many God-given gifts. Had he permitted it, most of us would have worshipped him. Some did, I believe, and that was a cause of much hurt. After years of careful thought I've come to my own conclusion—God gave Jim a healthy dosage of "frailties of the flesh" to help him. The spiritual side of Jim, the man with the power, was so tremendous that there needed to be human weaknesses to help him avoid being idolized."

Jim had seemed invincible, indestructible, almost awesome in his abilities and charisma. There seemed to be no problem big enough to defeat the man. He had led his people into the wilderness, passed through a "Red Sea" or two, and conquered the land. He had made Christ a living reality to thousands, pioneered a fresh, live movement within an often stagnant religious system, scattered disciples throughout the world, and taught his people the meaning of prayer, faith, and dedication. But in the end, he showed them his humanity.

As the tumultuous sixties rolled on, things began to collapse on Jim. Since October 27, 1937, the day something 'snapped' inside the pretty young girl he'd married, life had been a difficult road. Over a quarter-century had passed and Jim still lacked a solution. Maxine remained a crippled victim of narcotics. Finding an answer seemed hopeless, and Jim was near the end of his rope in dealing with this never ending nightmare.

Unable to sleep well, digest food properly or decrease the migraine attacks, Jim turned to sleeping pills in a desperate search for rest. With a surgically altered digestive system, too often these capsules would lay in his stomach overnight, then start to function during the workday.

At numerous public appearances Jim's speech was slurred and his message disoriented. On several occasions, he could not speak

154

at all. As word of these public failures spread, feelings of anger and confusion rose to the surface throughout Young Life. All eyes focused on 'the Boss.' "Is Jim on drugs? Has he lost his anointing? How could he do such a thing?" Sadly, there was far more anger than compassion.

Jim had understood his staff's devotion as love, not realizing that for some he was a father figure, for others a hero, and for others a spiritual giant who could do no wrong. He was emotionally vulnerable to his flock, and he never dreamed that his coworkers might turn on him.

This was such a tragically sad situation. Jim was still the anointed man of faith he'd been for years. His burden for the world's adolescents was bigger than ever, his love of Christ unaffected. He was funny and cute as he'd always been, and with his message of God's love he could still hold people's attention in the palm of his hand. His spiritual sensitivities were still peaking, but his deteriorating health and the weight of Maxine's problems wore as lead weights around his neck, and he was beginning to stumble.

Clearly, Jim's staff and board of directors had a sensitive problem to address. It isn't an acceptable thing to have a leader giving unintelligible messages to important audiences. Further, there was no way of knowing if the next time Jim was to speak he would hit a home run, or strike out. Jim was careless with this situation and should have been confronted, but his strong leadership style made it very difficult for his staff to approach him regarding a personal failure. As his son I can say that his bark was far worse than his bite, but I had a privileged perspective as well.

Complicating the issue, Jim was stirring up the waters with his comments on institutionalized Christianity. From earliest days his heart was in presenting Christ as attractively as possible. He didn't feel one could teach about Christ in a ritualized way that bored people, and he felt that most churches were boring. He was not criticizing people, he was simply describing the situation, as he saw it, within the institutionalized church. He didn't feel it bore much resemblance to New Testament Christianity, and he was boldly stating so.

The problem was that many on Jim's staff had longed for the day when the institutional churches would be more accepting of them and their work with America's teens. Not only would it feel great to be welcomed into their fold, but it could be a real financial blessing as well. With his comments, Jim was upsetting the applecart. Jim, on the other hand, was going to say what the Holy Spirit was revealing to him. Money, although an ever present need, wasn't in first place in Jim's list of priorities.

In this atmosphere of internal questioning, Jim had rammed his adult lodge project past a reluctant board of directors. Says a staff member: "There's no question in my mind that Jim's adult lodge was the coup de grace as far as the board of directors was concerned. The argument put forth was that a sane mind could not have conceived such a project."

"For years," said a Young Life board member, "we had sat there and let Jim's leadership supersede the economic problems we had. Our respect for him and his love for the Savior was greater than our insistence that the mission be sensibly plotted out from an economic perspective. We kind of relaxed and figured, 'Well, maybe a mission doesn't have to be run like a business, even though it gives us some problems.' Eventually, we figured we'd have to close Jim out."

In Jim's mind, there wasn't, nor could there ever be, a concept like "closing out" someone from their life's work, especially if that work was one's calling from God. Such an act would be akin to kicking one out of his or her own house, or place of business, and interfering with that which God had ordained. It was totally unthinkable to a gentleman like Jim, that anyone, let alone a Christian, would do such a thing.

In authentic Christianity, we do not "close out" one of our own. If one of our family is hurting, breaks a leg, becomes ill, or grows old, it is our God-given responsibility to love and care for said member of the family. But there were many issues going on here besides the boss's health. One of his staff members analyzed other facets of the situation:

"Jim's board and staff had a tiger by the tail—he wasn't about to change his whole approach when he felt that God was leading him in other directions. Jim would say, 'I've got the board down my neck, and my staff is three months behind in salary, but I'm not stopping. We're not put here to sit around and atrophy. There are kids in Europe, Australia, Asia, Africa, and South America with virtually no chance to hear about Christ as they should, so that's where we're going.' Jim was committed to international expansion; his people weren't. Jim was building Trail West Lodge; his people didn't want it. Jim was telling the institutional churches what they needed to hear, but rocking boats in the process. So, they took control of his work and kicked him out. If that doesn't follow the historical norm, then I don't know much about history."

On May 5, 1964, Jim was called to Chicago to meet with certain members of his board of directors. Jim's journal:

> Another full day at office with the Advisory Committee [top level staff men]. Received call from two board members: I'm to meet them in Chicago Saturday. Sounded grim. I talked to my men about this—they gave their unanimous assurance that they want me in my customary office—will back me, etc.

A member of that Advisory Committee who was in Jim's office when the board members called says: "That whole nightmare is almost too painful for me to talk about, so I'll say this once and hope I never have to talk about it again. Jim knew that something was up when he received that call from Chicago. As I recall, everyone present that day gave Jim his verbal assurance of support—within the next ten days we were voting on a successor. With exception of George Sheffer, I can't recall that anyone supported Jim when the rubber met the road. Jim must have felt completely betrayed."

Jim's plane ride to Chicago was an ominous preview of events to follow. He wrote in his journal:

> Worked hard at the office this morning. Left for Chicago at 2:00 p.m. That was the roughest trip I ever made in a plane—through severe thunder showers and extreme turbulence—drinks and lunch trays were thrown all over—a real mess!

157

The ax fell on Saturday. By the next week, Jim was already an outsider. He wrote:

> 5/8: *This was an unbelievable night. I left this shocking, late night, futile conversation, virtually in a state of shock! I'm to be stripped of all authority, and begin a one-year sabbatical leave in August. Start summer as usual, but keep out of program and fade out of the picture by July 1st. Are these men qualified? Is there vision on the board? It seems, except for a few individuals, to have always been lacking.*

Jim immediately called a May 12 meeting of his closest staff in Denver. He was the only one legally authorized to call this group together. I will never forget his broken heart at the end of this horrendous day. He continued his journal:

> 5/12: *Called a meeting of my Advisory Committee in Denver. The same board members included themselves without communicating with me. Either tonight or in the morning the Advisory Committee convened without me, the board men taking over. They are not members of this committee and have no authorization to call it together. What is happening? IMPOSSIBLE!*

It is interesting to note that only two members of Jim's board of directors met with him in Chicago on the night of May 8th, 1964. He was virtually removed from Young Life that night, yet the other members of Jim's board had not met, not voted, and with few exceptions, had no foreknowledge of these events. It is disturbing to realize that the vast majority of Jim's board didn't even know his removal was being considered. The whole thing smacked of a clandestine, maybe illegal operation, carried out by a few powerful and influential men on Jim's board who were obviously driven by intense anger towards "the Boss."

The minutes of the national board of directors meeting, held at Franklin Park, Illinois, on June 3-5, 1964, show the board's thinking. An excerpt:

> "Mr. Hull inquired whether the whole matter of Jim's removal had come up suddenly. He said he had been con-

cerned for some time over Jim's physical condition, but that Jim now appeared to him to be a man without hope. He cautioned the group not to walk ahead of God. Mr. "X" said the purpose of the May 12 meeting in Denver was to clarify matters of Jim's health and administrative capability. The meeting was called by Jim, but Mr. "X" and Mr. "Y" requested a hearing since it dealt with the perpetuity in office of the executive director."

Mr. "X" said that he and Mr. "Y" had requested a hearing at Jim's May 12th meeting in Denver to clarify matter's of Jim's health, but legally speaking, Jim was the only one who could grant such a hearing, and he never received a request for one. Obviously, Mr. Hull was caught off guard by this sudden power play against Jim. He hadn't heard anything about it, nor had most of the other board members.

Numerous questions immediately arise: Who informed these members of Jim's board that he had called a meeting of his staff advisers? What moral or legal right did these men have to usurp Jim's meeting? As Jim was the only one who could legally grant a hearing, why was such a request never received? As Jim had been told on May 8th that he was soon to be fired, why were most members of his board unaware of such an action?

A close friend of Jim and Maxine says: "I was at those Denver meetings and came away deeply disturbed. First of all, the board men who were there had no right to be, in my eyes it was Jim's meeting and they took control of it. What bothered me most, however, was the talk about Jim that took place behind closed doors. It wasn't honoring to Jim, and it most certainly wasn't honoring to Christ."

Jim's journal continues the story:

Executive committee of the board (with advisory committee called in from time to time) met for an hour and a half WITH-OUT MY BEING ABLE TO FIND THEM. Finally I got with them and couldn't believe what was happening. I left this afternoon crushed—no one came to me! This seems now to have been the darkest day of my life. I must hang onto the Lord—"I will never leave thee nor forsake thee" is for me too.

On June third Jim was in Illinois for the board of directors meeting. His journal records:

> I read my statement to the board, then left. Not in all the last four terrible weeks has an executive committee member spoken to me alone. I must correct this before I give way."

The following morning, the board reconvened without Jim present. The discussion centered largely on Jim's mental health, the implication being that he was a very sick man. After lengthy discussion, it was decided to give him a token title and a promise that he could return to the work if he would submit to psychiatric treatment. Jim wrote:

> I was brought into the board meeting, after an all morning wait, and was told the executive committee had recommended that I keep my title of executive director, although on leave and with no authority. It's obvious to me that they plan to superannuate me at the end of the year.

During this stormy board meeting, Mr. John Carter had questioned the wisdom of removing Jim permanently. Mr. "X" responded "that the essence of the original intent was that the change be permanent." Later, Mr. Hull asked if the board really did want Jim back, provided his health improved? Mr. "Y" snapped, "Back as what?" He said Jim hadn't demonstrated administrative talent. Considering all that Jim had brought to the table over the years, his anointed leadership, etc., this was a rather shocking statement that clearly stated the new organizational priorities—administration.

Jim's board agreed to allow him and his family one more summer's residence at his much loved Lookout at Frontier Ranch. The project that had cost him so much, Trail West Lodge, was only ten miles away, and it had just opened its doors for the first summer of operation. Jim's emotions lifted some when the national conference for Young Life committeemen opened at this beautiful facility on July 20, 1964. The very next day, on his birthday, Jim was ordered out of Trail West, given a directive to pack his family and leave the Lookout, and told he was not to set foot on any Young Life owned property ever again. He was given twenty-four hours to comply.

160

This photo was shot about two months after Jim's work was taken from him (compare this photo with the previous one in chapter 14 to see the rapid decline in Jim's health once he'd been ousted). He is losing weight rapidly, appearing frail and emaciated. Later this day, Jim was ordered out of Trailwest (where this picture was taken). These were dark days, as well, for Maxine. She was bloated, and hopelessly enslaved to an out of control drug addiction.

What was going on here? How could such a thing have happened? What was behind this brutal display of corporate fisticuffs? Whatever else he was, Jim was certainly a gentleman, and this is not something one would do to a gentleman. This was brutal; it was mean-spirited, and it was veiled in secrecy as much as possible. I was an eye witness. As Jim's son, I was personally ordered off all Young Life properties for "as long as I lived." I cannot describe the trauma of that day, and it probably hurt Jim even more. It seemed our family was surrounded by insanity and hatred.

It is especially moving to read Jim's journal shortly before all of this took place,

"I awoke early for prayer and prayed for each member of my board, individually, by name."

Christ instructed his followers to pray for those who persecuted them, and Jim never stopped doing so.

Maxine observed:

"I have always felt that when a person is limping and needs help, there's only one response to the situation—to provide whatever help you're able to. With his failing health Jim was obviously in need of love and support from his family and associates, and in this critical hour of opportunity a movement was launched to remove him from everything he'd sacrificed so much to build. I was an eyewitness to the suffering this dear man went through; I had caused a lot of it over the years, and I honestly believe it would have been more humane had Jim been taken out and shot. I don't say that in a bitter or angry way—I just feel it would have been more honest, and it would have saved Jim years of untold suffering."

As his son, I saw my father's heart absolutely broken, and I saw his work, everything he'd built, taken from him, smugly. After all, Young Life was his baby. It was built upon the blood, sweat, tears, and prayers of Jim and his coworkers. Jim didn't own it in the secular sense, but he was anointed by God to build it and lead it. Young Life was his in that sense, and it was his to pass on, and his to participate in, at whatever level his health would permit, until his death. But his work and his properties, properties that he alone had believed for, as well as the name 'Young Life,' were simply seized from him, and never given back. To add insult to injury, it was all seized in God's name. A former staff man analyzed the situation:

"There's a pattern in history that shows us that men will start new movements to address the changing needs of the world. Then, bureaucrats come in and build an institution. That institution, born to express life, then begins to stifle life. Whenever we get to the place of saying, 'Wait a

minute, we don't want to sacrifice anymore—we want re-
tirement benefits, better fund-raising techniques, more
administration—we want this thing run like I.B.M.' When
we get to that point, we lose the guts of the cross, we lose
the adventure, and we lose the vitality of the faith."

There is perhaps nothing quite as ugly or distressing as when
people unacquainted with the anointing of God turn on one who is
under that anointing and proclaim their actions justified because
they're doing 'God's will.' Anytime we act in an unloving way, while
proclaiming our actions to be the will of God, we are behaving as
the Pharisees behaved, a group not exactly known for demonstrating love, or exhibiting God's will.

No, no one was doing God's will here. God does not will this
kind of suffering on people. It was planned and carried out by men.
Jim was passing through the darkest valley of his life, while the board
was issuing its final resolution:

"At the conclusion of this resolution, we reaffirm our
pledge to pray for and work for Jim's complete recovery;
praising God (as we pray) for what he has accomplished
through Jim as founder and leader of Young Life from its
earliest days to the present; and knowing that God has yet
greater things for his people, praying with faith and hope,
with trust and confidence, that Jim's body, soul, and spirit
will be in health and prosper; and that he will go from
strength to strength and be even more fruitful in this work
in future days."

Oh, the masks that people and organizations wear in public!
No matter how kind-hearted the secretary who wrote this into the
minutes, he was clearly not speaking for the small group within the
board who had rammed through Jim's dismissal. Jim suspected he'd
never be asked to return, that references to any future days in Young
Life were purely a placebo. He was absolutely right, but he never
quit hoping that his friends on the board would see the barbaric
nature of these actions and correct them.

In retrospect, these shameful events were most likely illegal. At any rate, they were certainly uncivilized, and unacceptable amongst mature adults, let alone Christians. But Jim was too refined to smear his work's good image by dragging this into a legal brawl. He was too kind and good for what was going on, and he usually misread things because of it. He remained always tempted to think the board might really ask him back. He knew better, he just couldn't put that hope to rest. As a result, he'd do everything the board requested of him, no matter how silly, especially when it came to seeing psychiatrists that Jim didn't feel he needed to see.

In truth, Jim was getting the run-around, "If this doctor finds you well, we might open the door a crack." When the doctors found him well, it was said that Jim had pulled the wool over the good doc's eyes. Like the love-starved person he was, he'd do anything to please that board. It didn't matter, the small group of men who'd ousted him were in control, and they weren't opening any doors to Jim Rayburn.

As the full extent of his exile began to dawn upon him, Jim's emotions collapsed. Within months, the man's health was at an all-time low; he was visibly suffering, slowly dying from a broken heart. In early August, his two sons-in-law visited him in Colorado Springs. Jim wanted them to see the new headquarters building of which he'd been proud, so he sent them over with his key, as he was not allowed to go himself. Jim's journal, August 9, 1964:

> That's when I found out they had changed all the locks so that I couldn't even get into the building. This was a very low time for me—the ultimate humiliation. Just about couldn't stand to think of "my outfit" doing that.

Imagine the deep disappointment, shock, and pain Jim was experiencing, just in realizing that these were his close associates who were doing this to him. Is this the type of Christianity he had instilled in his followers? Could his own people, "my outfit" as he called them, possibly think that the Lord he had presented to them would condone this type of thing? Had he given his life to no higher cause than this? His grief nearly overwhelmed him.

It is difficult to explain the animosity that built up toward Jim and his family. Perhaps it's that "posse mentality" that turns a law abiding group into a lynch mob. It seemed that one indiscretion followed quickly upon the heels of another. Each felt like a poisoned arrow as it hit. Jim's confidential files were searched, and other members of his family, including daughter Sue, were caught up in the frenzy to persecute Jim's family. Then, there was the ever present gossip vine. Over local and long distance phone lines, Jim was being slandered. Who was behind it, and why? He could never find out. Before long, most of his friends stopped calling, and old acquaintances acted nervous, cool, or aloof in his presence.

Jim seemed in a state of shock. This negative spirit in the air was a clear indication of the Holy Spirit's absence, and Jim was deeply concerned for his life's work. There is nothing more agonizing to a man of integrity than to find that his friends leave him alone, not because they are unaware of his suffering, but because they doubt his word. With the sudden disappearance of his most faithful friends and supporters, Jim was left alone with God.

To be wounded by your friends takes you by surprise; it is a bitter pill. Jim had once prayed to share in the suffering of Christ. Was all of this the answer to that prayer? Within a few months, he had gone from one of the most revered, respected Christian leaders on the world scene to a much maligned, discredited, tragically sad human being. His health had gone from bad to disastrous. He was in a state of despair, the hopelessness that overtakes a sane mind when it is pushed to the extreme in grief. Jim wrote in his journal:

9/28: *Had a fine time with my Doc (psychiatrist). He asked me to think about why I'm not suspicious about people, and why I don't realize that otherwise good people are capable of plotting against me. He said I was to think it over. I did.*

10/2: *The day of inexplicable terror! Doc called it an 'anxiety attack.' Had breakfast with Lanes, haircut, and then the big trouble. I was still shaking and perspiring so that I could hardly talk to my doctor, but glad he could see me in that state. The ONLY thing of this kind I have ever experienced.*

Notes: The power of the Executive Committee (on the board) should be limited with regard to firing or appointing a president. Perhaps we need by-laws that they must have a two-thirds majority of the Advisory Committee (close staff) recommending the move and that it could only be made at a regular or called Board Meeting with two-thirds Board approval, and every reason or 'charge' being carefully and openly presented to all.

When Jim contemplated fighting the board for his rights, his spirits soared. But he was also in a state of shock that some of his friends had actually done this to him, and it seemed he was frightened. He knew he couldn't take much more but he wasn't sure if the attack upon him could be stopped. He couldn't decide whether to please the board (visit doctors and stay away), or fight back. As he wrestled with the issue, his emotions vacillated:

10/5/64: Appointment with Dr. Nelken. He surprised me by 'insisting' that I should go to the Board Meeting and before that lay plans for getting the reins back in my hands—okayed my proposal that I should then become active head with only Bill reporting to me until I feel like taking on more. Very encouraged.

10/27/64: Roy came at 9:30 a.m. We were together for over 10 hours. He was a great help and blessing to me—couldn't have been finer—still the net result left me disturbed and unable to feel certain, as I have the last few days, that I should go to Dallas and make a "fight" for my position. Roy feels it poor odds of success at this time—but if I decide to fight, he will go along. I am contrite before God at my downcast spirit.

10/28: A bad day, except for some good, though brief, time in prayer and in the scriptures this a.m. When, O Lord when, will come the end of this, and how shall I speed the day—while ever trusting You?

Although removed from the Young Life board of directors at the June meeting, Jim could scarcely believe that this action wouldn't be corrected. At this time, the name Jim Rayburn was synonymous with the name Young Life. Jim was Young Life, and Young Life was Jim, in terms of public awareness. One could no more ethically kick him out and off the board than to have kicked Walt Disney out of Disneyland. What was going on seemed other-worldly, an absolute impossibility in a civilized society, let alone a Christian one. Jim was in total shock with the whole affair.

He resolved not to fight the Executive Committee, believing instead that these men would have a change of heart, see the error of their ways, and correct their mistakes. Jim expectantly awaited an invitation to the Dallas board of directors meeting. It never came. His journal takes us to the end of 1964:

11/11: *A busy day in Chicago. I kept hoping I'd be called to Dallas. Two good hours of prayer in early morning. Life is rough for me in these, the darkest of my days.*

11/12: *Another day—sitting on the forlorn hope—not sure I can stand much more of this. Oh, merciful Father . . .*

11/23: *This is the best day I've had since that terrible knockout blow on May 8th night. Am angry again for the first time in months.*

11/24: *This was a great day! Peace and actual happiness. I had one and a half hours alone with the Lord in a very rich time, and a grand talk about it with Maxine. Haven't had prayer like that in two years! My Doc told me he doesn't think I'm sick. Neither do I! A wonderful day. Glory to God.*

11/25: *Tired but happy—and all my confidence is in the Lord, as much as is in me! Put more capacity for trusting you in me, Lord Jesus! I'm feeding upon the Scriptures—devouring passages. It must be the joy of the Lord again, as so often in the good old days—before May 8th. May 8th is my May Day.*

11/26: *For third day straight I got into the Word for some rich stuff. Prayer the same—it is like the old times, say ten to fifteen years ago. The Lord God has laid His hand upon me. I am beset behind and before, but the old things are new. It cannot but come right!*

12/4: We are immersed in beauty, but our vision is not clear. A good day with my doctor. He says they call me liberal—radical—a boat rocker. I wonder why not one board member gave me personal counseling regarding what I call "charges against me?" The erosion of power having once begun develops a momentum of its own. In light of recent experiences, I fear for the future of Young Life.

12/31: What a very, very difficult year is closing. My constant prayer—Oh God of loving kindness and tender mercy—may there not be another so bad—by Thy Grace, may 1965 be a wonderful year—made so by remembering, "Lo I am with you always." With Thy enabling grace may I find, and do, the Will of God—and truly LOVE the brethren and all men!

Into All the World

JIM'S vision had been to reach the world's young adults, the next generation, with the glorious message that God's Spirit can be known personally, and that the secret of this discovery can be found in the birth, life, death, and resurrection of Jesus Christ.

He looked at it like this—if God can be personally known, then what on earth could possibly be as important as that? If the claims of Christianity are true, then mankind really has something to celebrate! If the loving, kind-hearted, amazing, awesome, beautiful, creative Spirit-Source behind this unfathomable universe has really made it possible for us humans to commune with Him, then we've all got something to sing about, shout about, and put on our dancin' shoes about. There ought to be one grandiose news special coming on right now . . . We interrupt this program for this special announcement:

> *God has appeared . . .*
>> *He was beautiful . . .*
>>> *We killed him . . .*
>>>> *He rose . . .*
>>>>> *His Spirit is alive and eternal . . .*
>>>>>> *He needs a new body for his earth purposes . . .*
>>>>>>> *You're it!*

Now, that's a news story worth the air time!

Jim didn't just think that story was true and he didn't just hope it was true; he believed it was true with all his heart. Getting the word out to precious kids before their open, unspoiled minds would close was Jim's burden, cause, and purpose. In his eyes, there wasn't any other job. His was the only game in town.

Now, almost overnight, Jim found himself with no office, no staff, a shattered reputation, poor health, and precious little money. He felt like a man whose children had shipped him off to a home for the aging, saying dear old Dad was "over the hill," no longer an inspired leader, and no longer of much benefit to them. Far better to be rid of him, put him out of sight and out of mind, lest his condition be an embarrassment to all.

When Jim wrote in his journal that he feared for the future of his work, his fear was real and not without foundation. He knew that in the corporate world people are not always treated in a kind and loving way. It's not uncommon to fire someone who's given a lifetime to the company. Jim never dreamed that "his outfit" would seek to emulate the American corporate model. Jim had built something unique, more of a modern version of the New Testament ecclesia, but not a corporation. And in a Christian group, one cannot discard people because their health is failing or their usefulness to the corporate cause has diminished somewhat. When one calls his or her group a Christian group, there is an inherent responsibility to treat everyone involved with the group in a loving, respectful, highly ethical way. Jim never thought of "his outfit" as a corporation. In a 1958 message to his staff, Jim put it in his own words:

> Let's look at the Young Life organization for a moment; I am rather proud of it. We are organized (an organization) principally because in our world, with the tax structure being what it is, we could hardly work together and receive money out of a common treasury without being organized. We are not organized to gain membership. We are not interested in blowing this mission up until it has 10,000 staff people. We do not ever believe that is the answer. WE ARE NOT AN ORGANIZATION IN ANY SENSE except that it is necessary for us to be. We are actu-

*ally individual witnesses for Jesus Christ. Being banded together
in an organization doesn't mean at all in our own hearts what it
might mean to people out in secular society. The fact I am in a
group that has an incorporated name is something unfortunate
that has come into our culture. But we are engaged in the pri-
mary mission of the church . . . . "go and tell, be witnesses for
me."*

The treatment Jim was receiving surely wasn't what one would
expect from those who believe in love, even to the point of loving
their enemies. On October 28th of 1964 Maxine wrote to George
Sheffer, one of the men from Dallas Seminary who joined Jim early
on in building Young Life. George and his wife Martie were dear
and loyal friends, and Maxine was asking him if there was anything
he might do to stop the harassment and facilitate a more humane
treatment of Jim. In his sad response to Maxine's letter, George stated,
"The entire procedure relative to your husband has been one of the
most difficult that I have been connected with in my entire life. For
many hours I have prayed and meditated over it. Confusion seems
to persist in all relationships within the organization." Several para-
graphs later George continues, "Maxine, believe me when I say, I
have plead the cause of Jim more than any person knows except
Martie. At this point, due to what I have been instructed, I can say
very little. We love you and Jim and always will remain your faithful
friends."

In a letter to Jim's board of directors, one of his psychiatrists
clearly stated that the actions of that body were detrimental to Jim's
well-being. He went on to say that continuation of such treatment
would most likely cause an early death. This letter was virtually
ignored. The executive committee of the board said the doctor was
incompetent, and that Jim had 'shrunk the shrink.'

For years we tried to arrange a desk for Jim at the new Young
Life Service Center building (called 'headquarters' in those years).
We requested a small out of the way area in the basement, but there
was no room there for Jim; no official response was ever forthcom-
ing. The following journal excerpts serve as a sampling from 1966
through 1969, and echo the pain of these dreadful years:

12/12/66 *A very disappointing and shocking Young Life mailing list letter in the mail—almost all of it is FLAGRANT PLAGIARISM using my original statements of policy, language and ideas from my letters, and unacknowledged quotes from my speeches. It was a terrible day. I wonder if I can take even one more day like this. My spirits and ability to work greatly improved for 8 consecutive days until smashed down again today.*

8/30/67: *I'm so confused, despondent, unable to move out and get my ideas under way. Sometimes it's almost like 'strangling.' I must get some air or I'll die. And yet I don't—and the succession of near worthless days continues . . .*

3/6/1968: *Why is everything so hard? I pray and long for the inner peace and joy of the Lord—have for so long. Is this Ephesians 6? No one is throwing Christians to lions these days— maybe this is the "suffering" for now, or for me. Oh Lord, I need a let-up on it . . .*

4/28/68: *A most difficult and almost desperate day. What reason? Couldn't study or rest, and found no satisfaction in reading. Gloomy, near to despairing—regarding the future. Feel that I am "dying of creeping despair." And how long has this been so, but for brief intervals? I talk to the Lord about it. Before God I feel ashamed. He has made me know that I want His will above all else . . . and yet this repeated, perennial falling into such despondency. Oh, WHY?*

8/5/68: *The worst day of my life—this morning in family room— struggling to tell Bill Taylor and Maxine that I wouldn't make it—no time left—what to do with me, etc.*

11/29/68: *Being "out of my job," not knowing what to do, seems very hard on me. I am sad and despondent most of the time. The isolation, and being ostracized by my long-time co-laborers and friends(?) is the hardest thing to take. Am keeping it all before the Lord, as best I know—but it's not going very well.*

1/6/69: *This has been one of the most difficult days in years and that is saying a lot. A good bit of the day I was sick but could not put my finger on any physical reason. Some aches would not account for it. But, as always, trying hard to pin down the reasons, I think they are: 1. Indecision as to what to do—job, office, contacts. 2. Fear . First that no help arrives on any hand, no guidance from above—that I can discern, perhaps even "money problems." And the tragedy of it is that all these things can and should be conquered by a simple childlike trust in the Savior. I cry to him. I hear no answer. Bewildered!*

Interspersed between these tragically sad diary entries Jim continued the pursuit of taking his life's work overseas. In the end he did his work alone, as he had in the beginning. There had been no kudos for him and Maxine in Chama, New Mexico, and there would be no public recognition for loving kids in San Juan, Argentina, Karachi, Pakistan, or Campinas, Brazil. But Jim felt he had a job to do, broken heart or not, and he gave himself to that endeavor with a fullness of purpose that transcends human understanding. Having almost no help, and very little money, his efforts were never really known or publicized. But he would one day die knowing more kids by name, in more countries, than most people will ever visit.

One of the hardest things for Jim to hear after founding Youth Research International in 1966 were the numerous comments by some of his former staff that "Jim didn't really care about kids abroad, he was just out to prove himself to the Young Life board of directors." Fact is, Jim had no need to prove anything to anybody. It was a shameful, insane period in the history of Jim's work, and there was no stopping the attacks upon him. Imagine being foolish enough to say that Jim didn't care about young people!

By the late sixties Jim had friendships with kids and adults alike in Norway, Sweden, Germany, France, Turkey, Pakistan, Malaysia, India, East Germany, Argentina, Peru, Japan, Brazil, and several countries in Africa. He conceived and raised money for a kids' resort in Brazil; a follower, Diether Koerner, was working with him full-time in Peru, and a group of twenty college kids in Argentina were crazy about him.

In 1968, thinking he might move to South America, Jim took a crash course in Spanish at The American Institute For Foreign

Jim befriended this picturesque citizen of Hamburg, Germany, traded hats with him, and asked for a picture. His new friend enthusiastically accepted.

Jim, hamming it up on a train in Spain. He'd been a high school cornet champion in Kansas but had no ability to play a guitar.

Trade (the Thunderbird School) in Phoenix, Arizona. It was a tough course, designed for young men and women, and Jim was in no shape for the rigors he'd embarked upon. It is a wonder he finished the course. Much later we would learn that he had driven to this school, taken the required courses, and driven back to Colorado, while unknowingly victimized by a brain tumor. His journals express concern and worry that he could not remember vast portions of the trip:

> *3/27/68: Left Colorado Springs this P.M. and drove to Las Vegas, NM. All easy, fast rolling. Glad to get on with the next project. (Appended later: After arrival in Phoenix I could not remember this portion of the trip at all—no memory of landmarks, towns, etc.) (Later, 5/15/68: I still don't know where I*

stayed in Las Vegas, even after looking on the return trip. What does this mean?)

On May 10, 1968, his meticulous journal records,

"Graduation Day! We were drilled, grilled, examined—'pummeled' from 7:30 a.m. until 8:00 p.m.—my day began at 5:30. Then, tonight, speeches, graduation diplomas awarded, etc. Am too weary to write—Never did anything so intense! Nor anything that demanded such concentration. Great satisfaction to have completed it."

Jim completed the 'Key Man Course' and hoped to move to Argentina to establish a kids work there. He was so proud of his new found skills in Spanish! Like a kid with a new toy, he relished every opportunity to demonstrate his speaking skills . It would make most of his hearers smile as Jim talked slower than molasses (try to imagine the late, famous movie actor, Jimmy Stewart, speaking Spanish). The Thunderbird school had tried to speed him up, as is evidenced by this April 6, 1968 journal entry:

Had the regular two-and-a-half hours of review of the week's 15 dialogues, by two of the conversation teachers. Proved that I am keeping up and getting it. I certainly didn't know throughout the week. It is a blur. Of course I speak too slowly. They want me to speak Spanish faster than I have ever spoken English.

I walked with Jim in some remote parts of this world, saw his compassion and concern for people, and felt the sincerity of his heart. He was a man cut from the mold of the apostle Paul. For Jim, there seemed no river too wide to cross, no mountain too high to climb , and no village too remote to reach. Language barriers were just an obstacle to overcome. He was a man with a light in his eyes, a man touched by the Holy Spirit. His journals show the extent of his travels and echo the concerns of his heart, a very lonely and broken heart at that:

Pakistan—*To Khyber Pass this morning. Had the most wonderful heart-to-heart talk about the Lord and the faith for three hours tonight—alone with Ibo. Was worth the whole trip. How greatly he needs me, he has "no one else to talk to." How I long for and pray . . .*

Pakistan—*Another heart-searching talk with Ibo through the night. I must get all people I know who really pray to remember this dear kid and his family. To bed late. I am weary, thankful, deeply affected, and so anxious to know what we can do for kids in these dark lands. I cannot just act like they aren't there.*

Turkey—*I'm nearly cracking up because of the farewells—how amazing, surprising, and warming to be so needed, and wanted, by these dear kids. It is the same with all.*

Sweden—*Am so concerned for the kids here. They are all pretty well stranded—don't know any "alive" Christians. Another special stop in terms of friendship and expressing my sincere desire to help them.*

Argentina—*About 9:00 p.m., in very isolated country, we got stuck. The worst situation I ever saw. Water was running into the car. An hour or two later five swell guys going fishing stopped to help. They got stuck too. Eventually, we were all out and rolling again. Then an hour filling in a washout. Had crackers for dinner. We are eight-hundred kilometers south of San Juan— perhaps the most beautiful country I've ever seen—even prettier than Malibu. Found a peninsula that beats anything I've seen— what a place for a kids' resort. My head is swimming with plans for Argentina.*

Brazil—*Such attractive kids here. Met tonight with twenty-four of them—a small number but what a far cry from several years ago. What to do? How to get leaders? Why doesn't anyone want to go to them? The camp is beautiful—there's nothing like it in Latin America. The burden of Christ for these precious young lives is on my heart—like a lump in my chest. Oh, father, show me what to do . . . I go on, abysmally lonely. Why must it be?*

Jim's final trip abroad came in March and April of 1969. Together we traveled to Mexico, Peru, Argentina, Chile, and Brazil. In San Juan, Argentina, twenty-five college men had a fiesta in our honor. Jim wrote in his journal:

> *Jim III and I were guests of honor at a big fiesta today. This was one for the books—bestowing their highest approval, friendship, and honor upon us. I'm sure such a thing had never before been done in San Juan. It got pretty rough, due to all the toasts to us—seemed interminable—but of course it's a gesture of friendship. After all those toasts, they uncorked the champagne—boy, we were lucky to get out under our own steam. We both made it. I must write more about this historic event. It's this sort of thing that keeps pushing my insides—makes me sure that we can do a great job down here, and that we must. But how? Where do we find our people?*

I had never before seen a group of Latin Americans have such fun with two "gringos." Jim's charismatic personality had conquered another group of kids, seven-thousand miles from home. They didn't know of his exile, nor would they have cared. They only knew that he was interested in them and had traveled many miles to be their friend. Kahlil Gibran seemed ever so appropriate:

> *Truth visits us led by the smile of a child and a lover's kiss, and we close the door of our tenderness against her and abandon her as one unclean. The human heart asks succor of us, and the spirit calls us, but we stand as one turned to stone, hearing not nor understanding. And when one hears the cry of his heart, and the call of his spirit, we say that such a one is possessed of a madness, and we cleanse ourselves of him.*

Homecoming

JIM'S health was rapidly deteriorating. His journals from 1966 to 1969 record frightening symptoms:

> *Strange and scary symptoms with my eyes—can't always focus on the television, and see colored spots where I know there aren't any.*

> *Feel I have two lumps in my body. One is in my heart, and one is in my head.*

> *Seizure about 9 p.m. while watching television. Next awareness—ambulance—hospital.*

> *Very ill—worst time with my eyes—absolutely no focus possible—then seizure—hospital.*

> *I know something's wrong—my memory very poor—sometimes nonexistent. Cannot remember last two weeks. Frightening . . .*

> *Had my "hay baled" and speech prepared, but I took fifty minutes to present a twenty-minute message. Can't understand what's happening .*

At times Jim would tremble so violently we had to hold him down, but he had an inner quiver we couldn't still. He frequently

179

mentions in his journals those "terrible, terrifying inner shakes," something that seemed to be triggered by the trauma of his exile, a physical response to his overwhelming sadness. Who could say for sure? When Jim was visiting kids abroad, or dreaming of another property he wanted to build, these hellish tremors would subside. But when he contemplated the hateful way he'd been treated, those tormenting muscle spasms would take possession of his too frail body. This sweet, burdened man was physically and emotionally incapable of dealing with what had been done to him. He tried to take his sorrow to the cross of Christ and lay it down, but he simply couldn't get this accomplished. And this too, was a torment.

Sometimes these "inner shakes" terminated in a grand mal seizure. The most traumatic incident for me was the time he went stiff as a board while still on his feet. I bear-hugged him as quickly as I could, but nearly fell down trying to manage his stiffening body. What is one to feel when he holds a convulsing father in his arms? Jim was such a dear, kind, considerate man, and to see him like this was simply heart-wrenching. Why? For what? What had he done? Who had he hurt? What was his crime?

If Jim was on the road, with the kids, or otherwise working, his improvement was remarkable. But most of his time was spent at home, and it was not a happy, healthy, place. Maxine's emotional problems had entered their fourth decade, and Jim had no strength left to cope with the situation. A healthy, vibrant wife, a devoted and wise helpmate, might have put Jim back together a bit after his work was taken from him. Maxine, still deeply mired in the quicksand of her depression, wasn't well and couldn't help him. On average, five days out of seven she spent in a drug-induced fog. Jim had no strength for it, and no understanding of it. As a family, we'd tried everything we knew to help Maxine, to no avail. Her situation seemed hopeless. When we hospitalized her, sometimes forcibly, the doctors always found her normal and sent her home. We were at a loss.

Jim was the personification of humble, and it is only natural that he sometimes blamed himself for the bankrupt marriage he and Max shared. But as a child growing up in the home, I never saw Jim as anything but a model husband in the way he treated her. He was tender, sweet, and affectionate, what most women dream of in a husband. His patience was undying.

Even though Jim's world had crumbled in upon him, and even though his strength to endure further stress was at an all time low, never did he speak of Maxine in a disrespectful or angry way. From the time I was a little boy right up through my college years, Jim always said that she was not the Maxine he had married, not the girl he had known, but a woman he loved, buried by an illness we couldn't understand. "You must never harbor resentment in your hearts towards her," he would say to his kids, "she is suffering from a psychological illness. She is not her true self."

In almost every respect Jim was a broken man. There were nights I sat up with him while he searched for answers. The trauma of being kicked out of his calling was ever present in his mind, a terrible torment that would never leave. Sometimes he would cry, repeatedly asking me, "What have I done? Why have they done this to me? Where are my people?" I had no answers for him. What could I say? I didn't know. I was a very young man, just out of my teen years, and I had no idea that Christian people were capable of causing such torment as my father was experiencing. I wanted so much to help him, but I couldn't find the key.

When speaking to another about Young Life, in spite of its rejection of him, Jim never stopped using the word "we." Further, even though "his outfit" had disowned him and locked him out, he continued to raise money for his work with a dedication difficult to comprehend. What a strong statement about his character!

After five years of tears, trauma, tremors, and convulsions, we finally got the big news, Jim had cancer. On June 7, 1969, he wrote:

> *Dr. Beadles came by the room this morning and said I could leave the hospital if I want to. He said to come by his office Monday and by then he'd have the pathologist's report. It sounds fishy and ominous. I know very well that he got the report before he finished the surgery.*

Then, two days later:

To Dr. Beadles' office today. He beat around the bush— finally told me I have a prostate tumor, already spread to the bladder and urethra. It's a malignancy of a virulent type. I felt sorry for Bob [the doctor]. I told him he didn't need to horse around with me—just to give it to me straight. It's bad! Not much chance, medically speaking. Strange and wonderful—the measure of peace I had. I've felt worse about a broken leg.

After five weeks of cobalt radiation therapy there wasn't much left of Jim. Constant nausea, inability to eat or sleep, and those ever present tremors, all worked together to make living out each day a special challenge. I will always wonder if the radiation treatments Jim was given weren't excessive. His journal of June 16:

Began Cobalt 60 radiation today. Maximum level of tolera- tion, for maximum length of time tolerable. They didn't tell me what their computers said that would be.

Never again could Jim sleep normally, experience intestinal regularity, or feel even half way normal, if only for a few hours. He mentions that his insides felt burned up. His life became a living hell, emotionally and physically. His journals reveal a sad and des- perate search to find his Heavenly Father's hand and comfort. He felt distant from God and it bothered him constantly. Then, this rare but wonderful entry in his diary:

September 29, 1969—For years I've been praying that God would grant me great prayer experiences, as so often before. Under the most difficult and unlikely circumstances IT HAP- PENED—not much sleep, but prayer, earnest, longing, clinging prayer, repeatedly—almost constantly throughout the wakeful times—and, though so desperately burdened—the peace—a deep inner peace. Nothing like this since 1964! 5 years. "Oh, God . . ."

Unthinkably, on October 31, 1969, our family was jolted once again. Jim and Maxine's second daughter, Sue, age 29 at the time, had a breast removed, a radical mastectomy. Cancer had now struck two of us within five months. To the Rayburn family, life seemed a black hole. We were living through a night that had no sunrise. I'll never forget being with Jim when he heard the news about his daughter. He looked at me with desperate, unbelieving eyes, put his head down on his desk, and started to sob uncontrollably. I thought his heart would break into pieces. After this dreadful day, except for one brief entry, Jim never again wrote in his journal.

Knowing that his death was imminent, representatives of Young Life invited him to speak at an international staff conference in January, 1970, at the Asilomar Conference Grounds, Monterey Peninsula, California. It would be Jim's first appearance

Jim and Maxines' daughter Sue as she appeared when stricken with cancer.

before the whole staff since he'd lost his work, five years and seven months prior.

Hours before his message, Jim seemed on the edge of dying. His body wracked by pain, nausea, and radiation sickness, there seemed no way that he could speak. We in the family were most concerned with the consequences if he went ahead. But there were things he wanted desperately to say, and at 8:00 a.m. Jim stood before "his people." He was greeted with a standing ovation. I'm sure that tears flowed from many faces, as they did from mine!

Jim was funny, as always, recounting his days in New Mexico and Arizona. He told about the time he'd had to coach both high school football teams in the county, as there was no one else to do it, and about the day those teams played against each other. He said he nearly died from exhaustion running back and forth across that field. Then, when the laughing died down, Jim got to the meat of his message:

Everyone has a right to know the truth about Jesus Christ,"
Jim told the staff. *"They have a right to know who He is, a*

right to know what He's done for them, a right to know how they
relate to that, a right to make their own choice of Him.

Now, if you got in here accidentally, without realizing that
that's what Young Life is all about, then you ought to get squared
away, or you ought to hunt up the nearest telephone booth and
ask for the bus schedule. That's not just what Young Life is all
about, that's ALL that Young Life is all about—Jesus Christ.

Jim wasn't trying to sound poetic. In his years of banishment
he'd seen "his outfit" preoccupied with the institutionalized church
and Young Life's relationship to it. As the years would roll by there
would be other social and theological issues that would take center
stage for awhile.

It seemed to Jim, at times, that issues had become the focus
more so than Jesus Christ being the focus. For sure, something very
strange had come to Jim's work, and Young Life was changing. Further, some very gifted and talented leaders of young people were
now playing the role of corporate executives, trying to run things
like a business, as the board of directors had requested. Something
intangible, something very special and unique to Young Life got
lost in that shuffle.

Jim was telling the Young Life staff to return to their first love,
Jesus Christ, and the taking of His Gospel to young people in terms
they can relate to. Jim's work hardly needed theological debates and
theologians to define positions and immerse the staff and volunteers in their concerns. Jim was saying, "If you're on staff and you
don't realize and accept that's what Young Life is about, then get
the bus schedule, find a bus, and take leave!"

Seemingly, few "heard" what Jim was saying or took him seriously, as the issue previously mentioned stayed an organizational
focus point for years to come. Further, Jim no longer had authority
to enforce his viewpoints. Sadly, after his message, it was "back to
the status quo."

One joyful interlude in these otherwise difficult days gave Jim
quite a lift—finding out that Lucia, his Brazilian daughter-in-law,
was expecting a baby. "It will be a girl," Jim said, and then he an-

nounced to the family that he'd made one last major request to the Father—that he would live to see his granddaughter. None of us thought he had a chance, but if Jim had said that he'd asked his Father for a red-nosed reindeer, it would've been wise to prepare the corral.

There was a freshness, a little boy realness to Jim that endeared him to people. Frequently at the Penrose Cancer Clinic he'd pick out a despondent looking person and greet him or her with, "Hi, how are you doing with the cancer today?" After the shock wore off, a few engaged in their first open and honest conversation about their illness, exposing their fears and soaking up the warmth of Jim's personality.

Thanks to John Miller, Jim had been given access to Trail West Lodge. Outside of the Lookout, there was no place in the world he loved more. At times during his last months, Jim just needed someone to talk to. One night at Trail West, John, the manager, was awakened by a knock on his door. Groggy and confused, John glanced at his clock, saw it was three-forty-five in the morning, and assumed he'd been dreaming. After a brief pause, the knocking continued. John struggled to his feet, grabbed a robe, and clumsily made his way to the door. His eyes fell on Jim, leaning against the door casing, "Hi, John, don'tcha want some ice cream?" "Yeah," said John, "I've just been lying here wishing someone would ask me that."

Jim did live to see his granddaughter, Shannon Kathleen. When Lucia and I left the hospital with our newborn baby, we took her straight to Jim's bedside.

Two factors came together to produce this radiant picture of Jim, not long before he passed on. Firstly, he was at Trailwest Lodge, a place he absolutely loved. Secondly, the work crew there had just showered him with love and appreciation. Emotionally, he'd been like a dry sponge needing water (love) and when it came his way, he glowed.

185

He held her in his arms but didn't say a thing. The moment held great significance, for in the eyes of that baby girl, Jim saw that God had honored his final request. Now his time was up.

Ten days later, Jim had a sudden burst of energy. He got up, got dressed, arranged transportation, and went to say good-bye to several old friends. Then, on the afternoon of December 7, 1970, while napping, I dreamed that my father had come to the house, sat on the bed, and laid his hands on me. I was informed on waking that he had come, and done as I had dreamed it. I have no doubt that he was praying, and saying good-bye. It would be six years and four months before I would fully understand what had taken place there as my father prayed for me. He prayed well.

Late that evening, December 7, 1970, the nurse called to inform me that Jim had taken a turn for the worse. Within twenty minutes I was by his side; it was too late for any final words together. Just that morning he had talked to Maxine of another dimension. Now, so soon, he was beyond our reach.

Jim had suffered another seizure, vomited blood, and lapsed into a coma. His breathing was heavy, and an awful "death rattle" was clearly audible. I'd never seen someone die; I didn't know there was a "death rattle." What a dreadful sound!

Harlan Harris, a minister and long-time friend of Jim and Maxine, came to Jim's side immediately. Harlan read aloud a passage from the New Testament, and without opening his eyes, Jim mumbled, "I know that one." It gave everyone there a nice, needed laugh. It was the only sign of consciousness he gave; he never spoke again. To this day, I find this simple thing, Jim being funny in the midst of a deep coma, to be that which symbolizes so much of his life.

We had promised my father that he could die at home and that we wouldn't lengthen his final hours in any way. Not wanting him to fight for breath, we ordered a tank of oxygen. Morphine was given on schedule.

Seconds turned to minutes, minutes to hours, and hours to days. The only sound was Jim's labored breathing. He'd been an unhealthy but strong old mountain goat and he wasn't going to go anywhere without a fight. After forty-eight hours of listening to him labor for air, in spite of the added oxygen, I felt I couldn't take much

186

more. I went off to pray, asking God to give me some indication, when the end finally came, that He was there, that Dad was with Him, and that things were in His hands. It didn't seem to be the case.

On the morning of December 11, 1970, after eighty-one hours in a coma, the rhythm of Jim's breathing changed dramatically. He labored to take his last breath, held it briefly, and graduated to his higher destiny. He had slipped beyond the reach of further suffering or pain. Deep sorrow and deep joy blended into one. Borrowing words from Martin Luther King Jr., "Free at last, free at last, thank God almighty, he's free at last."

Within seconds, a flock of birds just outside the open bedroom window burst into song. And they kept on singing as if their little hearts were filled with joy. "An early summer morning," I thought, "not at all like December. Thank-you, Lord."

The emotional trauma and isolation of Jim's last six and a half years contrasted strangely with the hundreds of tributes which poured into Colorado Springs from around the world. A sampling:

"Jim now knows fully what we still know only in part. We rejoice with him. I am grateful for the privilege that was mine to know him, and to experience his unique gift of teaching a group to see Christ, above and beyond all. I pray that today, again, through Jim's death, as through his life, we will focus our attention and message on Christ, above and beyond all else."

Kay McDonald, staff member

"So Jim has gone with God. Alleluia."

C. Stacy Woods

"The sympathy of me personally and of Inter-Varsity Christian Fellowship to the Rayburn family and to Young Life over the death of Jim Rayburn. He was a godly man whom the Lord greatly used. May the comfort of our Savior be yours this day."

John Alexander, President
Inter-Varsity Christian Fellowship

"We thank God for the life and ministry of our beloved brother, Jim. We shall miss him."

William Culbertson, Moody Bible Institute

"We send our deepest sympathies to the Young Life family, especially to Maxine. Rejoicing in all God has brought into being through Jim's vision and commitment."

Bruce Larson, Ralph Osborne,
Heidi Frost, Wally Howard, Faith at Work staff

"Am glad Jim Rayburn is now in the arms of Jesus. He was one of the greatest Christians I ever knew, and he had a profound influence on my life. He had suffered a great deal in recent years, but I'm convinced that it is only through suffering that we can share in the glory of Christ. It is now up to us to carry the torch Jim so courageously carried for so many years."

Billy Graham

"The Y.F.C. family extends deep sympathy, and yet rejoices in the triumphant passing of our beloved brother, Jim Rayburn. It is our prayer that his large vision shall find increasing fulfillment."

Sam Wolgemuth
Youth for Christ

"Rayburn's life was an inspiration to all of us. He fulfilled life's noblest purpose in leaving a heritage to the world. It would be impossible to evaluate the immense impact which this man had upon the lives of others."

Frank Morrison
Governor of Nebraska

"Our mutual friend meant more to me than can be expressed. He taught us the practice of love by example. He made Christ a reality, a true companion and friend. Our love and prayers are with his family."

Doug Coe

"It was sad news to learn that a great man will no longer be among his friends on earth. Jim Rayburn's life expressed the real victory in living for Christ."

Albert H. Quie
Congressman from Minnesota

"How we thank the Lord for the ministry Jim had on our work. He was truly a pioneer for Jesus Christ."

Lorne C. Sanny
Navigators

"Jim realized the necessity of communicating the gospel of Jesus Christ in language intelligible to this generation He was one of God's tools to shape me for service."

George M. Cowan
Wycliffe Bible Translators

"Jim's passing brings vividly to mind a great summer at Star Ranch in 1950. My life could never be the same again. I am so deeply grateful that I was allowed to know Jim Rayburn."

William T. McKenzie

"Jim did something unique in Christian history, I am sure. He was God's instrument for pulling my life out of a confused aimlessness to purpose, enrichment, and love. How I thank God for him! I wish he'd been granted more years of useful, creative work, but wow, didn't he give us a whale of a lot?"

Bob Page

"I am sure there was a great rejoicing when Jim passed on. Many who were there through Jim's teaching were waiting for him. That includes our son, Tom, who went home to the Lord at the age of sixteen while in camp at Star Ranch in 1948."

Walter and Jean Henderson

"On the night of February 23, 1952, Jim, under the guidance of the Holy Spirit, spoke to my heart. That night I met my precious Savior. Our little guy, Mark, at five years of age, went to be with his heavenly Father on October 27. He had a rare blood disease. It is only the Lord who sustains us."

Ron and Emily Huber

"My loving sympathy to the Rayburn family and the Young Life community in this day of common sorrow and grateful remembrance. He who is now with the Lord he so dearly loved and served, and whose vision brought into being one of the most original and dynamic mission projects of our time, will live on in Christian history as one of the great saints and evangelical pioneers of this century."

John A. McKay
past President of Princeton Seminary

We awoke Sunday, December 13, to find the following article on the front page of the *Colorado Springs Sun*. It was written by Bill Woestendiek, the editor, in his column, "Thinking Out Loud." He had met Jim only once, and conversed for an hour or less:

Jim Rayburn never got his book written, but he got his life lived and made thousands of other lives better because of his. Jim died Friday at 61, and the people of our town, and young people everywhere, lost a good friend.

I was lucky enough to meet and talk with Jim only last week. He called me and asked me to come by his house and chat about things he considered important: our town and our young people.

As many of you know, Jim was the founder of Young Life, an international, interdenominational, interracial movement that has "turned on for the Lord" thousands of young people around the world. Young Life has been described as "friendship evangelism," and has given disinterested teenagers not only an intelligent look at the Christian faith, but a new outlook on life at a time when they need it.

Jim, 61 years young, sat in his living room last week, his body wracked with the pain of a killing cancer, his eyes bright with joy, and he told me why he started it. "The kids needed it, they were responsive as the dickens to it, there was nobody else who would do it if I didn't, so by George, I thought I'd take a crack at it."

What a crack that rugged man took at it! In his words, "It's almost too big for its britches now." The story of the growth of Young Life and what it has done for many kids who needed help is an interesting one, but this is about the man who started it all, Jim Rayburn.

"I wanted to talk to you," he told me last week, "because I like what you're trying to do for this town, your fight against drugs, your efforts to help people."

And I wanted to talk to him because he already had done so much for so many people. I asked him if he saw many changes in today's kids.

"It's an entirely different ball game," Jim said. "It's so changed you can't believe it. We've dealt with tough kids all our life. We take them as they come . . . . Rich toughs are harder than poor toughs . . . . But we didn't have any of this drug problem." He shook his head sadly. "Now, you can't believe it."

He straightened up in his chair, grimacing, but his voice was firm. "It's responsible for major changes in our work, but it doesn't change our effort. Any kid on any level, no matter how much of a smart aleck or how far out he thinks he is, we'll accept him, and we care in terms he can understand. If we can't do it, we'll take the blame."

"They told me I wouldn't live until last June," he said slowly. "But I had to see my granddaughter. I didn't say grandchild," he emphasized, "I prayed for a granddaughter. And she's beautiful."

Jim's nurse was leaving. "You just keep sweet now," he told her. Concerned that we were talking too long, I asked Jim how he'd sum up his life.

"I was trying to give kids a chance to take a crack at the Christian faith. This involved either believing it or not, they're free to make a choice. But it's hardly fair for nine-tenths of the

people to be making their choice on the basis of some mutton head college professor's book or something, with no exposure to it at all. We want to give them a chance to exercise their option."

Jim exercised his option to the hilt. He died filled with a concern about people and the problems of our town that worried him more than the killing pain that wracked his body. He wanted to talk about our problems, and what the Sun could do about them.

"You have the guts of a grizzly bear," he told me, and I shall long treasure that remark. But Jim was dead wrong. He had it all backwards. He's the guy who had "the guts of a grizzly bear." I thought, as he insisted on walking me to my car, and stood in the sun waving good-bye, that it would be beautiful if we could do half as much for as many people as Jim Rayburn did in his all-too-short young life.

I am grateful that he called me last week. It was an important afternoon in my life.

Healing

SHORTLY after Jim's death, Max decided to take up dancing. She gave herself to that with an enthusiasm she'd never shown for anything else. In short order she was entering dancing competitions from Puerto Rico to California. In so many ways, she seemed on the mend. Then word arrived that daughter Sue had inoperable cancer in both lungs; five lesions in one side, two in the other. It didn't seem possible; only thirteen months had elapsed since Jim's death.

Sue died on July 3, 1973, at the age of thirty-three, after a long, painful, and bravely fought battle against this merciless disease. Between Jim's passing and Sue's, Max had flourished as never before. And she had made such progress! But the trauma of losing her daughter so shortly after losing Jim had been a serious setback. Emotionally, Max crumbled. For the next six years we lost her again to the tyranny of narcotics.

In the spring of 1979, in a heavily sedated state, Max suffered a bad fall, cracking her forehead open on the edge of a cement stair that led into her house. Several hours later, she called to say she needed help. I arrived at the scene of a nightmare. Blood was everywhere—the porch, the carpets, walls, windows, even the refrigerator. Mother's head was split to the bone from her right eyebrow to an inch above her hairline. She was confused, and her pulse was faint. I rushed her to the hospital and had her sewn up in the emergency room (fifty stitches), but I couldn't find a doctor who'd admit her. By now, Max had a reputation amongst the doctors and no one wanted to get involved. I reluctantly drove her home and put her to bed. My prayers seemed to fall on deaf ears. Oh, merciful Father, how long?

Things went from dark to pitch black, in a hurry. The very next day, Max fell again, nearly killing herself. I had taken several ambulance rides with her over the years as we raced against cardiac arrest from a drug overdose. But I had never seen, or imagined, anything like this. I found her head split open, again, in a gruesome, horrifying injury. It was a ten-inch gash, open to the bone. Both eyes were black and her body was badly bruised. The house looked like a murder scene, and Max looked like a victim of gang violence. As no one was with her when she received these terrible injuries, it remained a mystery how she had hurt herself like this.

She was desperate, pathetic in appearance. She'd look at me with those confused, needy, desperately sad eyes, and I felt helpless to assist her. We'd tried everything to help my mother, for roughly forty years! The problem had absolutely overwhelmed Jim. More than anything else he had longed for and prayed for a cure for Maxine, and he had died without a solution to this, his greatest burden.

I was despairing in my prayers for my mother, "Oh Loving Father . . ." With the help of Dr. Donna Johnson, a childhood playmate, friend, and gifted psychologist, I admitted mother to the psychiatric ward at Penrose Hospital. Caught in this tangled web of sorrow, Max had hit the bottom of the barrel. She was at the low point of her life. It seemed like a nightmare without end.

Anybody who doesn't believe in a devil should have seen Maxine. The Bible reveals that Satan's intentions are to destroy, steal, and kill. He had certainly declared war on Maxine, back in 1937 or even prior, and by now he had destroyed her marriage, destroyed her health, destroyed her family life, stolen her youth, stolen her joy, relentlessly attacked her husband, and stolen her daughter. It appeared that now he was intent on killing Maxine, and he had nearly done so by the time I checked her into the hospital.

There was something deeper going on here than Maxine simply needing to find the Lord. She knew the Gospel, in the way so many Christians do. She had even served as a substitute teacher for Jim's Sunday school class when he was away. People valued her input. In fact, her intuitive perceptions into the things of God were at times remarkable, if only for their simplicity and purity. Even in the darkest years of her illness, when lucid, she had penned insightful and poignant poetry, such as follows:

A Bitter Thing

Jesus said, "I thirst."
Then they came and offered Him
Vinegar mixed with gall,
A bitter thing.

Cruel jest of hate,
When Jesus craved a drink
They came and offered Him
Vinegar mixed with gall,
A bitter thing.

Had they but known
It was not Christ who had
The greater thirst,
Though ardently He craved a drink.
Their dry parched souls
Did thirst the more for living water!
Their mocking eyes did look upon
That fount, and could not see!
So blind,
They came and offered Him
A bitter thing,
Which He refused.

The cup He drank was black and foul,
A cup of anguish, caustic,

> Grievous, far more bitter
> Than vinegar and gall.
> The cup of darkness that He drank
> Was wormwood! and
> He drank it all!

Yes, Maxine knew the Gospel. All mixed up and entangled in this dreadful dependency on drugs was her inability to dance with organized religion. Wheat and tares grow together. There is a counterfeit Christianity, and although Max couldn't define it as that, she could see it and sense it, and she tried but couldn't conform to it.

A recurring dream best illustrates Maxine's struggle, "I was outdoors, on a high, forested mountain ridge, and there were lots of people around me. Everyone was busy, running around looking for something, and they were oblivious to my presence. Finally, several approached me and said, 'You'd better get busy, Maxine, there isn't much time.' I said, 'For what, what's happening?' They said, 'Oh, Maxine, there's going to be a big, big masquerade party. We're all going; we're all in it. We're trying to find our costumes so nobody will know who we are. We've got to have good costumes! But Maxine, you're just standing here—don't you want to join the fun?' I said, 'No, look!' and I pointed to the ground. We were standing in a beautiful green meadow with lush strawberries, but people were running around and trampling them, oblivious of their actions. I was amazed, angry, and frustrated. I wanted to stand up tall and put a stop to the whole thing right there! But I didn't."

The religious masquerade had bothered Maxine ever since her introduction to Jim's boyhood home—yet, it was also there that she had learned fundamental things about history (His story—God's story). The problem was the Good News (the Gospel) was all mixed up with the bad news (religion, rituals, rules, and legalism). As Maxine had been a newcomer to the whole scene, she couldn't sort it out. If truth be told, most Christians today don't have it sorted out. We believers have gotten way off the track here and there, and we've mixed so much in that Christianity today hardly even resembles New Testament Christianity.

What true Christianity is basically all about is coming to the end of ourselves, and submitting to Christ's Lordship, and letting Him have the lead in our lives. The process of dying to our own egos and our own ways, seeing and confessing our substantial unbelief, and submitting to a Spirit of love in hopes we can come to see Jesus Christ in our fellow man, doesn't come easily.

The event that Jesus referred to when he talked of being 'born again' is the most wonderful, special thing that could ever happen in one's life. It's like getting a new set of eyes and a brand-new brain, one not quite so uncomprehending. It's being introduced to another dimension in a very real sense, the dimension of the spirit world. It's like getting it signed, sealed, and delivered that we can spend an eternity with our Father, whose only desire is to love us forever. Further, any others of our family and friends who have submitted to Christ's Lordship will be with us as well, and our Father has put His seal on it!

It's a hard package to beat! Imagine, it is the desire of God's heart to give us every good thing we've ever wanted, and in His time He will do it. And it's ours to have? All this is really ours to have? Yes, absolutely free, to you and me. But it cost God everything. Who wouldn't take a deal like that? Ah, but not so fast. Like Maxine, we have to come to the end of ourselves, first. This is the battle of life here. This is the war of wills. People don't die to "themSelves" easily. Going on with our story . . .

Max had felt from the first day she'd been exposed to it that something was wrong in all of this "Christianity," all this religion that had gone on around her. She'd felt something was missing—LOVE. And in the end she'd been proven right.

"The emotional trauma of Jim's last years," she recalled, "had served to convince me that my intuitions had been right, that I should have listened to them more carefully. There are a lot of wolves in sheep's clothing. I knew something was wrong, badly wrong, but I didn't know what the solution was. It wasn't in my nature to stand up and tell everyone to take off their masks. I've always hated to hurt people's feelings."

One can only imagine what benefits would have been available to Maxine, her children, Jim, and the Young Life staff, if she

197

had stood her ground. But she was a shy, timid, and insecure person who lacked confidence in her own intuitions. When she saw a problem, she waited for someone else to confront it. Her writings over the years show a spirit veiled by a constant heavy-heartedness:

Longing

Peace and quiet—for this I longed.
So young,
So immature,
I longed for peace and quiet.
Healthy children played
And made such noise,
I longed for peace and quiet.

The years sped by -
The children grew
And went away.

So now alone
The peace, the quiet that I longed for
Is here.

Now older,
More mature,
I long to hear the children's noise.
The sound that healthy children make in play
Is not a burden,
Cannot be compared to the loudness of the silence
I now endure.

To Sue

(Jim and Maxine's daughter, who died at age thirty-three)

You came to Rest
   upon the bosom of my breast -

some years ago -
    I loved you so!

Little beauty—like a flower
    your fragrance passed -
    and made me glad -
    every sad and painful hour.

Dear one—now rest
    upon His breast,
Just nestle down in Him -
    He loves you now—and
    He loved you when -

You came to rest
    upon the bosom of my breast -
    some years ago,
    I love you so!

Things are not always as they appear, especially in the spiritual realm. I drove home from the hospital where I'd left my mother and felt a discouragement beyond words. She truly had the appearance of having been beaten by a gang and left for dead. Although I'd never seen her quite this way, I'd also never known her any other way than drug-dependent. I was thirty-three years old at the time, and I'd never seen her well. It had become a hopeless situation.

So many true Christians can tell you that they had their most life-changing encounter with the Lord while at the very bottom of the barrel. Christ said he hadn't come to save the righteous, but those who are lost and broken. Nothing stands between God and we human beings so much as our own egos, so the process of having our egos destroyed is essential to spiritual growth. The proud will not be seated at the Lord's banquet table.

I cannot say for sure what the last barrier was to Maxine's spiritual breakthrough, but I can say that there was no ego, and no pride, left in her as we admitted her to the hospital. She was broken in every way. Her injuries were so severe, and her spirit so low, I wasn't even sure she would live.

As horrific as things seemed, we Rayburns were about to receive some awesome news, news so good it's hard to find words that describe it. Something wonderful happened to Maxine that very first night in the hospital. It was the dawning of a new day and the answer to many years of prayer. The Holy Spirit, the Comforter that Jesus promised His followers, came to Maxine in a powerful way, showing her compassion and freedom like she'd never imagined. He just shed a new light of love upon her and she was never again the same.

As surely as Jesus Christ called Lazarus from the tomb, so He did when He introduced Maxine to the dimension of the spirit realm, and freed her from the bondage of drugs. Ironically, as she was being set free from this demonic dependence, she was also being released from her battle with religion, freed at long last to be at peace with her intuitions. And in the end, those intuitions had been 'gold' all along. She had spent the better part of her life resisting a religious masquerade and looking for the real thing. Did the Lord ever show it to her! Max spent one night in the hospital and checked herself out, a new person, her true person. She continued to write poetry, but with such a different tone:

The Holy Spirit and Dancing

If the Holy Spirit
    had His way
There would be
    nothing but Jesus
and dancing.

If the Holy Spirit
    had His way
    in my heart
there would be
    nothing but Jesus
and rejoicing.

If He had His way
in the world
there would be
nothing but truth
and loving -
there would be peace
singing and dancing
If the Holy Spirit
had His way!

Max was an altogether new person. In a 1982 letter she wrote that "Today, my life is like a continuous state fair. As Elizabeth B. Browning wrote, 'Earth is crammed with Heaven and every common bush is afire with God, but only he who sees takes off his shoes.'"

It was wonderful to see my mother like this! This was a wholly unexpected, glorious gift of God. Maxine was a new creation—not perfected by any means. But she was raised up, laughing instead of crying, praying instead of complaining, reading and discovering in-

One might call this a picture of the Holy Spirit. It's the new Maxine, drug-free, joyful, at peace, in her early seventies. Max continued to look this way to age eighty-five.

stead of worrying. She was at peace with life, enjoying it, and happy. I had quit believing that I would ever see her this way. Oh, what a joy-giving experience to see a crippled mother get up and walk. Thank-you, Father, Thank-you!

Maxine had not 'gotten religion,' as the saying goes. Not at all. In fact, she'd gotten rid of it. She had met the risen Christ, the Christ of the Spirit realm, not just a theological Christ in some seminary textbook, or a sad, dull, lifeless Christ as pictured on many car dashes and church bulletin boards. The Christ Maxine had met is alive, and they communed with one another, daily. She'd call me, my sister Ann, or my wife, Lucia, and tell us of these times, and we'd talk by the hour. Had she become religious? Absolutely not! When asked what kind of man and woman God was looking for in raising up the work of Young Life, she responded, "I don't really know. But I know what He chose. And many years later I know that if God could use Ballam's ass, He could use Jim and I."

If one needed prayer it was a wise old owl who'd enlist Maxine. Frequently broken-down by severe arthritis, she felt that prayer was her role in things. That, and watching television. And Max could pray the bumps off of logs, nearly. I remember her being most self-conscious about a large bone spur that appeared on her knuckle. It was quite unsightly, as well as bothersome. She always kept one hand folded over the other when anyone was around, so they wouldn't notice this disfigurement. One night she went to bed with a simple, childlike prayer that her Father would remove that thing from her hand. When she awoke her hand was normal! No kidding! I saw it. If answers to prayer come from simple, pure, childlike faith, then Max was left holding the keys, as that describes how she prayed.

Ironically, way back before her illness, before Dallas Seminary, out in the wide open spaces of the Southwest with Jim, she had once simply made the suggestion to him that they kneel by the bed together and ask God to cure Jim's migraine headache. According to her, they did, and that was the end of the matter. The headache vanished. If her memory is correct, whatever had gone wrong? She was a new Christian, remember, and full of a childlike faith.

From 1980 till 1997, Max lived out her days in a mobile home on the east side of Colorado Springs, Colorado. She was quite at home in her very humble circumstances, and very much at peace with her life. She traveled some, visited some Young Life camps and get-togethers, painted a little, wrote some poetry, and watched a lot of television. In between, she quietly blessed a lot of lives with her profoundly effective prayers.

Excerpts from the author's journals, which seem to say it best:

11/21/1997, Friday: *Today was one I shall never forget, and somewhat traumatic. A call from Mom's neighbor informed that she wasn't answering the door, or the phone. When I arrived it took a few minutes to get in cause it was locked up tight. Gained entrance through the backdoor window. Found Mother fallen over the toilet. I've no idea how long she'd been there, and don't even like to think about that. Fortunately, she doesn't remember any of it. She had a major stroke that left her paralyzed on the left side and unable to speak well. Worse, however, the brain scan showed a significant mid-brain hematoma that will take her life. The emergency room physician said it could be hours, or it could be days, but he gave no hope of a recovery. The brain surgeon said there is nothing that can be done. This is it . . .*

11/22/1997, Saturday: *Spent most of the night at Mother's bedside, from about 1 a.m. to 7 a.m. Came home for a couple hours of sleep. She is in pretty bad shape, although she does communicate some through squeezing my hand and feebly mumbling a few words from time to time.*

11/23/1997, Sunday: *Went back to the hospital at 1 a.m. and stayed till 8:15 a.m. Was alone with Mother through the night. She is about the same but slowly weakening. We are giving morphine every three hours or so, and she can have it each hour if it is needed. She hurt herself when she fell and grows fidgety when the medicine wears off. As the hours roll by she slowly slips away, becoming less and less responsive. Tonight it is only the oxygen that keeps her alive. I told her today, while she could still hear me, that if she saw our dear Lord Jesus, to go with Him. Shannon was with me and in a better position to see her eyes than I was. Shannon said she teared up immediately. It is so sad, cause*

203

she can't do a thing for herself. She could never call the nurse, ask for anything, adjust anything, etc. She is totally helpless, and unable to speak. May God shorten these difficult hours, and carry her into paradise with a royal welcome, is my prayer.

11/24/1997, Monday: About 4 p.m. we transported Mother to the Pikes Peak Hospice at St. Francis Hospital. She was pretty unresponsive most of the day. She is now off of the IV, weaker, and with a fever. Her time is shortening. Love oozes from the walls at the hospice and I'm glad she's there. Tonight Shannon and Michelle have gone there for the night. Shannon just called and Mom is sleeping restfully. Several times today the difficulty of this hit me, as it did Lucia, and Ann. Ann is pretty broken up. Dying is not easy, and it's not pretty, but all in all, I think this is far and away the most peaceful 'death process' I've seen— an answer to prayer. I cannot imagine mother living longer after this devastating stroke. Lucia and I are pretty exhausted tonight.

11/25/1997, Tuesday: Was at the store for about two hours only. The rest of the day and most of the night was spent at the hospice. Mother continues to slip away, but ever so slowly. I've a tendency to worry about her comfort, thirst, etc. and hours of concern start to add up and become emotionally draining. The whole family seems tired and testy tonight. Mom is still hanging on. It's been five days now. The folks at the hospice are wonderful, and a godsend.

11/26/1997, Wednesday: Spent most of the day with Mother. Bless her heart—it's just a very slow decline into unresponsiveness. Today I no longer felt that she was aware of my voice, or presence. I'd drop water into her mouth but she didn't even move her tongue. Her color is still good and her circulation is fine, but she's no longer with us. Tomorrow is Thanksgiving, her favorite day, and she was planning to come. I'd be thankful if it's the day of Mom's entrance into heaven.

11/27/1997, Thursday: Perhaps the hardest day on us yet. We found Mother somewhat more responsive this morning. I talked to her quite a bit about letting go and going with the Lord, that *when she sees Him, not to worry about things here, but to go with Him. When I asked her to always pray for us, she tried desperately to speak—three times she made a high pitched sound. When I saw her more responsive today I was nearly overcome with a need to feed her, give her drink, etc. It is so very hard not to worry about her comfort, whether she is desperately thirsty, etc. I pray that she's comfortable.*

11/28/1997, Friday: This day will be forever etched in my memory. I went to Mom's bedside about 10:20 a.m. The minute I arrived I knew this would be the day, and that I'd need some moral support. I called the family to come right away. Mom's breathing was labored all day, the 'death-rattle' increasing as the day went on. It was very difficult to be around, frankly. She seemed comatose, or I'd have gone crazy listening to her fight for air. What a difficult day! The last hour she seemed like she had stopped breathing several times, only to start up again. Near the end I prayed, committing her spirit to the Father, put my hand on her heart and said 'be still, be still, be still.' She took another breath or two and stopped breathing. After the trauma of the past week I felt such tremendous relief. Six and a half hours have passed now, and I still feel relief and joy that this dear woman is now with the Lord. What a week it has been—eight days actually. It is over. Praise God!

As she requested, Maxine's body was donated to the University of Colorado Medical School. Her husband Jim and her daughter Sue had also donated their bodies in like manner. Maxine left the following, something she had credited to a Robert N. Test:

> *The day will come when my body will lie upon a white sheet neatly tucked under four corners of a mattress located in a hospital busily occupied with the living and the dying. At a certain moment a doctor will determine that my brain has ceased to function and that my life has stopped.*
>
> *When that happens, do not attempt to instill artificial life into my body by the use of a machine. And don't call this my deathbed. Let it be called the Bed of Life, and let my body be taken from it to help others lead fuller lives.*

Give my sight to a man who has never seen a sunrise, a baby's face, or love in the eyes of a woman. Give my heart to a person whose own heart has caused nothing but endless days of pain. Give my blood to the teenager who was pulled from the wreckage of his car, so that he might live to see his grandchildren play. Give my kidneys to one who depends on a machine to exist from week to week. Take my bones, every muscle, every fiber and nerve in my body and find a way to make a crippled child walk.

Explore every corner of my brain. Take my cells, if necessary, and let them grow so that, someday, a speechless boy will shout at the crack of a bat and a deaf girl will hear the sound of rain against her window.

Burn what is left of me and scatter the ashes to the winds to help the flowers grow. If you must bury something, let it be my faults, my weaknesses and all prejudice against my fellow man. Give my sins to the devil. Give my soul to God.

If by chance you wish to remember me, do it with a kind deed or word to someone who needs you.

Prophets

PROPHETS come in different shapes and varied sizes. They are easily recognized in history books, seldom appreciated in their time. Historically, prophets have been unquestionably controversial, and at times, unpardonably hostile. They've always been people who announced, pronounced, and denounced. Most have met with persecution, and a "untimely" death. Like Jim, they have usually been at odds with the established religious system. Prophets are God's anointed, and mankind's enigma. Jim may well have been one, but it's not for a son to say.

In essence, Jim was the avant-garde leader of a church searching for its New Testament roots; it was a church two-thousand years new, a group of talented, diverse, lovable people who came together to sing, laugh, and pray (and how we sang, and how we laughed, and how he prayed!). This was a church without a chapel, but no chapel was desired. It was a church without an organ, yet music was its heartbeat. Outreach was its purpose, and prayer was its foundation. Christ was its Spirit, and Jim was its soul. In many ways, it was a church from the pages of Acts, and she was a beautiful bride.

A former Young Life board member, and dear friend of Jim, Dr. William F. "Chubby" Andrews, recalls:

"It is with a deep sense of love and great joy that I remember Jim and the many happy hours we spent together—at the ranches, here at our home in Memphis, when I was an intern in Chicago, and the time Jim spent a week with me at the hospital. I can genuinely say that much of the fruit in my own life's work has been by the grace of God through the influence Jim Rayburn had upon my life.

"It is my sincere prayer that those who have a love, burden, and concern for young people in their hearts, may again recall the enthusiasm, zeal, love, compassion, and selflessness that was manifested in the life of Jim. Jesus Christ himself, who Jim so wonderfully honored, will again be glorified and praised as the center of the work of Young Life."

Jim was a man who spent hours in prayer, who hungered for and sought his Lord's leading above all else. Although he acquired or built yachts, resorts, and kid's camps, whatever was needed, he himself would say, "How amazing to see how the Lord works, it's as if I do nothing!" He meant that too. Jim was genuinely, joyfully surprised that God would take 'an everyday sinner,' like himself, and use him to the degree that He did. Bottom line, Jim expected God to be true to His Word. When anyone walks in expectation of experiencing God's promises it is simply that expectation that powers the process. God's kingdom is real! It is actuated in one's life by expectation (faith). One doesn't have to bring anything to gain entrance to God's House (His Realm, not a church building)—just one's expectation, one's faith. That's all there is to do, that's all there is to exercise. How wonderful to realize that God created us with everything we need.

Even children have faith; they exude expectation. "Daddy's taking us to the zoo tomorrow! Daddy said it, I believe it, we're going to the zoo!" That's what Jim did, with a childlike tendency to believe that God would work in his life, answer his prayers, and be true to His Word.

A lesson everyone can reap from Jim's life is to enter into that 'magical, childlike place' of yielding one's life to his Father's care, and walking in expectation of seeing Him work. Jim exercised his childlikeness, and his Father responded! He will for everyone who trusts Him.

God asked us to call Him 'Daddy' (Abba). He's a great Daddy! The very best 'earth daddy,' absolutely the very best, is only a whisper of our Heavenly Daddy. The Bible teaches that no one, no one on earth, has seen, heard, or even imagined the glories of being with our Heavenly Daddy. This is what Jim wanted all kids to know, that they have a Heavenly Daddy who loves them beyond measure, and that Jesus Christ holds the key and leads the way to Daddy's house. He is the door to the mansion.

Jim's heart ached for people who didn't know Christ in this personal, life-changing way. That earnestness sets the man apart, and it also looms as the greatest challenge to those who would follow him. One will not emulate Jim, nor do the work that he did, on admiration alone. The Spirit that drove this man cannot be held within the confines of corporate structure or administrative excellence. To institutionalize Jim is to lose him, and everything he stood for. This issue will serve as the greatest challenge to the work Jim left behind, and history makes obvious the danger lurking.

Let's return to Jim's journal entry of December 4, 1964:

> We are immersed in beauty, but our vision is not clear. A good day with my doctor. He says they call me liberal—radical—a boat rocker. I wonder why not one board member gave me personal counseling regarding what I call "charges against me?" The erosion of power having once begun develops a momentum of its own. In light of recent experiences, I fear for the future of Young Life.

Jim was justified in worrying about the future of his work. For roughly thirty years after labeling Jim as a liberal, a radical, and a boat-rocker, Young Life wracked up one of the worst records imaginable when it came to loving its own people. When the treatment Jim had received wasn't deplored, and regretted, it set an appalling standard for how to treat people. Andrew "Goldbrick" Delaney, a dear individual who with his wife Gerry gave his all to Jim's work, said, "Young Life was never the same after that. When we saw what happened to Jim we knew that any one of us could receive the same treatment. That was the day a family became an organization."

As individuals, each of us is responsible to repent of our mistakes and hateful actions, especially when others are hurt by them; organizations are not exempt, they must do the same. When we (Young Life) didn't do so, we lost the love of Jesus Christ. We defended our actions and denied Jim's pain. And after he was gone, many more would pay the price for our insensitivity. It is ironic that a ministry known for its relationship skills with teens became so abjectly poor in terms of quality relationships within. It seemed the Holy Spirit had departed, leaving us spiritually bankrupt.

Jim's work limped along for years. In the corporate offices, sometimes issues seemed to be the focus more so than Christ and kids being the focus. At times, power struggles took center stage. Over the years, Star Ranch and Silver Cliff ranch were sold, hundreds of corporate executives came and went, various cliques fought each other for control, but the kids work survived, even if bruised a bit.

True Young Life work takes place at the bottom of the corporate pyramid, and everywhere a spiritually-sighted adult takes time with an adolescent and seeks to share God's love. Even though things had gotten bizarre at the corporate offices, we never lacked for altruistic people in the front lines, hanging out with kids. Thank God, that never stopped. And that can't be stopped, regardless of what happens with the corporation. That's what Jim was referring to when he suggested that after fifty to sixty years, perhaps his work should be disbanded. He was referring to the corporate part, of course. The spirit of his work, meeting kids on their own turf, building a viable friendship with them, sharing God's love with them in their language, while keeping it "alive" and interesting, that will never cease. That genie is out of the bottle.

Many things have changed since Jim was on the scene. A staff man, or woman, in Jim's outfit was not expected, or required, to wear so many hats. Jim simply wanted those who shared his burden for kids, and those who shared his inner fire to know Jesus Christ intimately, to spend their time in prayer, study of God's Word, and reaching out in a spirit of love to teenagers, no strings attached.

210

That was his job description for a staff person, a point made earlier in this book.

Sometimes it was a frustrating job, sometimes a lonely job, sometimes a scary job, and always a challenging job, but it carried with it the privilege of being exposed to Jim, taught and humored by Jim, and the very high privilege of walking in dependence upon the Lord's faithfulness to provide one's needs.

Jim constantly pointed out to his people that they had the lofty calling of sharing the most important news life has to offer with young people who might not ever hear it otherwise. It was a life of high adventure with God, and Jim kept his staff in touch with that. Salaries weren't guaranteed; Jim and his staff looked to God as the source of their supply in a way not really understood nowadays. Today, there is a tendency to look to a fund-raising banquet, auction, or golf tournament to supply the financial needs of the work. If truth be told, putting on an effective fund-raising banquet or golf tournament has become a key part of the job.

Money is a necessity, of course, and there isn't any evil attached to raising it, but there is something wonderfully exciting, and faith-building, in walking in dependency upon the Lord for one's daily needs. It's not an easy exercise, but it builds one's relationship with God like nothing else I know.

Young Life is most effective at the camping level; kids love a Young Life camp! Jim wanted kids to pay attention to his life-giving message, and he felt that removing them from their normal environment was vitally important. There are no boyfriends calling, sports practices, peer groups, parent problems, and other distractions at a Young Life resort. Kids are free to listen to the message of God's love for them, experience that love, and deal with their personal reaction to it all without external interference.

Another, and rather critical part of Jim's success with kids is that he took Jesus Christ out of the institutional church and its religious demeanor, and gave Him back the attractiveness and loveliness and realness that religion has robbed Him of. Kids and adults alike responded. One of the dilemmas future Young Life staff will face is the pressure that's been applied to them over the years to plug kids back into the very religious system that Jim had become so discouraged with. If a town is blessed with a group that's full of love, life, joy, and the Holy Spirit's touch, a group who's gatherings are virtual love feasts for Jesus Christ and one another, wonderful! But many Young Life leaders will not have such a marvelous option.

Quite simply, authentic Christianity is about Christ and a personal, individual relationship with God through His indwelling Spirit. It is not about religion, denominations, seminaries, rituals, clergy, organizations, dogmas, creeds, degrees, or even Christianity. There is a huge difference between Christianity and Jesus Christ. This is the very thing that Maxine had a hold of yet couldn't define. It is the very issue Jim was speaking out about more and more as he entered his fifties.

Christianity left the cradle of its birth and went to Rome where it became an institution. From there it was pretty much downhill. It went to Greece and became a philosophy. It went to western Europe and became a culture. It went to Asia and became a concept. It came to America and became a corporation. In each case it was changed from a relationship to a cultural tradition.

Jim Rayburn was another voice crying in the wilderness, calling people back to Jesus Christ. His only tool in taking this life-giving good news to young adults was his personal faith. He had no guaranteed salary, almost no benefits, no plan, few people, and precious little encouragement. But Jim gave to God the only things God really desires from any of us—a yielded life, and our trust!

Jim took Jesus Christ off the black and white pages of the Bible and placed him there in front of us for all to see. We discovered that He was wondrously attractive, far more so than we'd ever dreamed. Jim helped us to see that Jesus laughed, and that he still laughs, that Christ is also King in the realm of humor. And in our hearts we soared; God seemed closer. Laughing together became a part of worship, and a very major part of Jim's Young Life work.

Jim taught us that we learn more about God in climbing a mountain than we're likely to in an hour of church. In our hearts, we felt lighter; we've all been bored in the sanctuary, but days in the high country are savored. And he showed us where to look for the source of our power—on our knees. That was hard. In our hearts we rebelled, for we didn't really like to pray as much as he did. But he

212

challenged us, and his example is always in view. Jim seldom did anything that wasn't a thrill, so there is something in prayer we may have never discovered.

Emile Cailliet, author, scholar, and former Princeton Seminary professor, wrote of Jim:

> "He was one of the most unassuming, revered leaders of this century. I shall always have a vivid recollection of Jim— one that I will never forget. It was the time I saw him at prayer. His ruddy, infinitely kind face was lifted up, its features sharply outlined in light and shadow, like a Rembrandt portrait. The cares and deep concern of a fully committed

Emile Cailliet, Princeton Seminary professor, author, scholar, and dear friend of Jim, sent this picture to Jim that he inscribed 'For Jim, in a common vision of love—Emile, 1962.' Emile authored a book titled Young Life, *published in 1963. This photo was taken very near the spot where Jim was building an alpine chalet, above Frontier Ranch.*

life were writ deep in lines and furrows that gave him a weather-beaten appearance. Jim's whole being was in that prayer. When he had finished, his thin, muscular body was leaning forward in vibrant self-offering. His face, radiant with love, continued to pray long after his lips had closed, as if what he had to say could no longer be put into words. What an ineffable experience his prayer was that evening! I shall always think of it when I remember Jim."

Personally, I shall never forget a long, hot, miserable day that I spent with my dad in the interior of Argentina. The date was April 11, 1969. We had left Buenos Aires early in the morning on a flight to Rosario; our purpose was to rendezvous with several university students who had heard of Jim through an Argentine exchange student.

Shortly after noon we arrived at the designated meeting place, an outdoor amphitheater on the banks of the Paraná River. There being no trees at that location we sat in the hot sun for more than two hours awaiting the arrival of our "hosts." No one showed up. The mosquitoes coming off that river seemed to us like Texas blue jays, and it soon became clear that we had been selected for that day's lunch. The heat and humidity soared to heights that Colorado boys are not accustomed to; I thought we were going to melt, right there in the middle of Argentina.

In mid-afternoon, as we were just about to leave, a small group of noisy, boisterous college kids arrived to greet us. They weren't late, by Argentine culture; we'd been early. Being two "Gringos" in a foreign land, we had no idea what an Argentine means when he says, "We'll meet you at noon."

We were there to share Jim's dream of a great work in Argentina and to open the door a crack for discussions of Christ. But a couple of these kids were Jewish, and had no intention of letting us speak on such subjects. For some time they grilled us with questions about the Vietnam war, American politics, the Roman Catholic Church's domination of South America, and other complex issues. Firstly, we hadn't come to talk about those things, and secondly, neither of us could converse on such topics with our limited Spanish. We were depending on a young Argentine that had met Jim years before at Frontier Ranch to translate for us. But the Argentine young people had brought along an American student to do the translating, and he was a pugnacious sort who seldom correctly translated a word we'd said. He felt it his duty to protect his Argentine friends from these 'suspect' Americans.

Things couldn't have been more awkward. As these Argentine young people looked up to their American friend, our heated conversations with him (seldom translated) only served to decrease our rapport with the group. We were clearly in a losing situation; it was not an event I ever hope to repeat.

Our flight back to Buenos Aires was delayed; we stood in a minuscule airport till late at night, and were not back till the wee hours of the next day. We arrived at the hotel sunburned, bug-bitten, and exhausted. We both plopped down on the edge of our beds and stared down at our shoes, as if too tired to remove them.

Next thing you know, Jim lifts is head and starts to talk about what a great day it had been, how thankful he felt for the opportunity to know such a great group of kids, and how he hoped God would lead him in spending more time with them in future days. Being one of the worst days of my life, I climbed into bed without saying much, and drifted off to sleep wondering what possessed my father. It was a life-changing question. I'm so glad I asked it!

For you, Jim, these words from Theodore Roosevelt:

> "It is not the critic who counts, nor the man who points out how the strong man stumbled, or where the doer of deeds could have done them better. The credit belongs to the man who is actually in the arena; whose face is marred by dust and sweat and blood; who strives valiantly, who errs and comes short again and again; who knows the great enthusiasms, the great devotions, and spends himself in worthy cause; who, at the best, knows in the end the triumph of high achievement; and who, at the worst, if he fails, at least fails while daring greatly, so that his place shall never be with those cold and timid souls who know neither victory nor defeat."

Dance, Children, Dance

CHAPTER *20*

HIGH above Frontier Ranch, on a summit ridge of Miriam peak, nestled in a Bristlecone pine forest at the very edge of timberline, there sits in silent splendor another of Jim's ventures—a mountain chalet with an indescribable view and an open door to all who come upon it.

Jim built this alpine wonder in the early sixties, dedicating it in the summer of 1962. His journal from July 19 of that year:

A great day! Ninety of the committeemen took the trip up the jeep trail to join in the dedication of the "Mt. Princeton Chalet."

Taking work crew kids up Mt. Princeton over Miriam Peak was one of Jim's loves, and this remarkable chalet provided a base camp second to none. The view is simply beyond words. Further, he could pack up his guests and give them dinner, or the night, at a place like no other.

The property sits on National Forest Service land that Jim leased. The chalet is built of rocks taken from the mountain, but Jim would not permit those of us who constructed it to use rocks from nearby. He insisted that we haul each and every rock from at least a quarter-mile away. All of the water, sand, and cement necessary to mix the concrete had to be carried to the site as well. The support structure for the roof was made of lodge pole pines, and the

Such a telling photo. Dedication of Jim's alpine chalet, at timberline in Colorado. For Jim, a joyful, thankful, and proud day, another of his dreams fulfilled. By his whole demeanor, one can see his satisfaction, as well as his weariness. I can only imagine what Jim endured to get Maxine up that jeep road. Max was in 'the valley' here, a place she was destined to spend over 37 years. Bags under her eyes reveal her true condition. Jim, although happy and thankful, is understandably drained. He never gave up on Max, or quit believing for a miracle. This was far more like a mother and son than a husband and wife. A picture is worth a thousand words . . .

roof was finished off with cedar shake shingles. Dale Kaiser, an artist with such types of buildings, wore two hats: architect, and construction foreman. It was my privilege to spend several summers working alongside some great guys in actually constructing this remarkable chalet.

A most unusual thing about this place is that the door is open to all, and most who enter in get richly blessed by the experience of being there. This alpine shelter has saved many a wet, cold, mountaineer from the raging storms that blow across the high summit ridges, and it has welcomed many weary climbers who'd underestimated the toll of climbing a Colorado "fourteener" (a mountain in excess of fourteen-thousand feet elevation).

For untold climbers, this chalet has been a beacon of warmth and welcome in the most hostile of high altitude storms. There is no carpet on the floor, no art on the walls, no refrigerator or range, or mattress, or comfort—no toilets that flush, nothing we'd normally think of in an Aspen or Vail. Yet, few places have felt more like home to those who have stumbled in, inspired a greater awareness of God and His love, or touched people in the way this place has. The following is a sampling of writings left there by the general public, writings that could fill a book, and writings from people who never imagined their contemplation would be published:

> "You cannot stay on the summit forever—you have to come down. What is above knows what is below; what is below does not know what is above. One climbs, one sees, one descends. There is an art to conducting oneself in the lower regions by what one saw higher up. When one can no longer see, one can at least still know."

> "To See Thee more clearly
> Love Thee more dearly
> Follow Thee more nearly
> Day by Day"

> "Thank-You God for Your Wonderful Creation."

> "Cherry Creek High School Young Life. A wonderful two days in an amazing place. Hope the next people have as much fun."

> "Be Still and Know that I Am God."

> "Our family was climbing up to the peak and it began to hail, with lightening striking. To find this wonderful shelter and be reminded of the best within the human spirit is humbling. Thank-you so much. This is truly God's Country!"

"What an incredible spot to breathe in God's goodness. Blessings to those who built this place for others to enjoy. This time has marked a turning point for me. So, I'll always remember this 'alpine paradise.'"

"What a beautiful place! We really appreciate the shelter from a violent hail storm."

"We've traveled here from Maine. It's spectacular here, like nothing we've seen before. The beauty here connected with our souls. It was with these surroundings that Jason, my fellow climber, told me he wanted to marry me."

"Great solitude. Violent nighttime winds. Awesome sunrise. Peaceful morning. Squeaky mice. July weather in October. Perfect day to summit. God is Great!"

"There is no way to take all of this in and doubt that there is a God."

"I call as my heart grows faint . . .
Lead me to the Rock that is higher than I . . . Psalm 61"

"What a surprise to find this chalet! We are lovers in troubled marriages enjoying each other as never before. We arrived just ahead of sleet, rain, and vicious winds. Thanks for maintaining this great place."

"Nature is truly God's second Bible. We can seek His face at any altitude, any geography, but there is something beyond special about doing it above timberline on a Colorado 'fourteener.' Spent an extremely windy and cold night in this great mountain shelter. Snow is higher than the front door. I pray that all who enter and exit these doors will be blessed, and find all that they seek. God is the King of Kings and Lord of Lords. He is waiting to give all of us truth and wisdom beyond the realm of our realities. If you don't know

Him personally, ask Jesus, His glorious Son, to come into your heart and live forever. You'll be amazed at what happens. Just believe!"

"Came to spend the day in solitude, just being still and knowing. God, in His constant faithfulness, came along side me, embraced me, and reminded me Whose child I am. His promises are true. He never fails. Praise be to the Living God.!"

"Thanks Jim Rayburn. We are some happy, happy campers—escapees from summer staff at Frontier Ranch. It's foggy now at 1:00 A.M. We hope the sunrise is clear, and perfect. God is just too awesome for words!"

People don't leave that kind of writing, as a rule. It's usually "Kilroy was here," or "Joanne likes Tommy," or "Billy Joe loves Anna Jean," but one doesn't generally encounter writings like those above. What was it about Jim, and the things he left behind, that has this effect on people?

Those who have found a sense of God's presence at this mountain chalet have done so without a chapel or church building. Further, there are no pews lined up in neat little rows, no worship service programs, no pulpits, no organs, no pastor or priest in clerical garb, no stained-glass windows, no sermons to endure, and basically none of the normal folly associated with 'worshipping God.' At this 'outdoor cathedral' there is nothing more sacred about Sunday mornings than Friday nights. It is an inspiring place.

Like this beautiful chalet, Jim's influence on twentieth and twenty-first century Christianity continues to bless lives worldwide. For parents of teenagers, there are few words sweeter to the ear than, "Mom, Dad, I'm going to Young Life. See you later." For parents, those are wonderful words to hear! Those same parents might easily hear, "Young Life? Heavens no! I'm looking for other, more esoteric things on weeknights." Oh, joy . . .

In a world that feeds its children every kind and type of developmental poison, Jim's work continues to take the good news of

Jesus Christ's love to every kid who's searching for answers, meaning, or a sense of his own worth.

Quoting Kerry Alberti, a recent chairman of the Young Life Board of Trustees, "Young Life, the legacy that Jim Rayburn left to the kids of the world, continues to grow and flourish. In the summer preceding this book going to press, over thirty-three-thousand high school (and junior high) kids heard the gospel of Jesus Christ proclaimed at one of seventeen Young Life teen resorts. During the school year, over eighty-four-thousand kids from schools across the USA heard the gospel at weekly club meetings and smaller campaigner groups. Today, Young Life has over two-thousand-four-hundred full time staff people and over twenty-thousand volunteer leaders dedicated to Jim's vision of reaching every teenager with the very good news that Jesus loves them and died for them. The format used today is basically the same one Jim pioneered so many years ago—go where the kids are, build a relationship with them, earn the right to be heard, keep the gospel fun, exciting, and relevant.

"Jim Rayburn was our founder, although he never meant to found anything. He set the direction for a new concept of reaching out to kids who would never willingly attend church. He defined the process that we still use today of how to reach kids. Several decades after his death, Jim Rayburn's words can still be heard, quoted in Young Life gatherings, official publications, and informally among the staff. If it weren't for Jim Rayburn we would still be trying to figure out how to get kids excited about Sunday school."

It wasn't easy for Jim to hang around a high school campus, and it's not easy for the leaders who do it today. Jim would even joke that when driving to a school event, or even his Young Life Club, he often prayed that he'd get 'creamed' by an eighteen-wheeler prior to his arrival. Most people who have led a Young Life Club know the feeling. Thank-you, all!

As a boy, Jim had been deeply influenced by his father, James Chalmers Rayburn, who he called 'the best preacher I ever heard.' His father had instilled a hunger to know the Lord in his young son that was to bless countless thousands of lives. Yet, like so many preachers of his day, faith in the Lord Jesus Christ was all mixed up

222

with rules and regulations. Jim had been raised on the 'evils' of movies, card games, dancing, girls who wore makeup, and a hundred other things.

As Jim's faith matured over the course of his lifetime, he became less and less structured, increasingly distressed over the state of the institutional churches, and increasingly focused on Jesus Christ alone, as the Spirit of God freed him from the bondage of his past. And that's the key to spiritual growth and discernment—the Holy Spirit. A "Christianity" that leaves Him out is nothing more than a dead religion, a masquerade, and a charade.

One can read a book a week on the subject of God, graduate with a doctoral degree from a respected seminary, pastor a church, memorize the Psalms, host prayer meetings, lead a Bible study, serve as a missionary abroad, teach a Sunday-school, and author a book on Christianity, but without the anointing and revelation of God's Spirit, that same one will never know God as He wants to be known.

The Holy Spirit is the Spirit of Love, the Spirit of God. God doesn't care about one's theological education, or dedication to practicing religious rituals. He is not about that! He is about love, grace, truth, joy, and liberty! To worship God is not a service rendered, and no 'worship service' is involved. If truth be told, 'worship service' is an oxymoron of the first degree. To quote Jim, "Where did we get so far off the ball?"

To see these simple things through God's eyes, one must be touched by Divine Spirit. It's a prerequisite to knowing Christ in a true way, as the Holy Spirit manifests the person of Christ in human flesh, as us, and if we don't know that Spirit, then we only know Christ in a kindergarten sort of way. Perhaps we don't really KNOW Him at all. Maybe we just know a lot of things about Him. But our Heavenly Father doesn't want this. He wants us to KNOW Him, in spirit and truth (John 4:24).

It is time for we 'Christians' to stop preaching and practicing a dull and bone-dry religion, and seek the touch of God's Spirit. It is both ironic and shameful that most of we 'Christians' are best known by others for what we're against, how judgmental we are, the rules and rituals we observe, what denomination we support, what political stand we're taking, or what building we go to on Sunday morning at 11:00 o'clock. Seldom are we known for the love we express, or the joy and freedom we carry through life. Rarely are we even seen among those who don't profess Christ, preferring instead the comfort of the like-minded. That's not the way it is though, in God's kingdom. People who are filled with divine love for others aren't hanging around playing church. They are out on the highways and byways of life, as Jesus Christ was. They are the church!

Without the Holy Spirit, who reveals and produces the person of Jesus Christ in mortals, we are left with religion, a pitiful masquerade. Religion kills and destroys; Jesus Christ brings life abundant. The time has come for we Christians to take off our religious masks, and ask our Father in heaven to pour out His Spirit upon us as only He can do. And when we dance together in our spiritual nakedness, perhaps we will come to appreciate what Jim Rayburn said, "Jesus Christ has freed us from the curse of religion." *Alleluia!*

Dance, children, dance!

FATHER, it is finished. I give you back the laughs, the tears, the lonely hours, the precious insights, and the many miracles you have given me. May these words go forth to bless, heal, and inspire other lives, bringing them to a living consciousness of their oneness with you.

Unfinished Business in the 21st Century

THE JIM RAYBURN FOUNDATION

SINCE those days when Jim first modeled a unique, natural, and long overdue style of sharing God's love with young people, way back in the wilds of New Mexico and Arizona, God has preserved his work. Today, Young Life is reaching more kids than ever before. It continues to be a lighthouse in a sometimes dark and confusing adolescent world—a beacon of God's love to kids in a time of overwhelming social, physical, and emotional change.

Jim went home to God determined that every teenager in this world has a God given right, a birthright, to hear about the life of Jesus Christ, what He has done for them, and how they relate to it—not just to hear it, but to hear it in language intelligible to their culture and circumstances, such that they can make their own choice of Him. Jim called this his "Big Dream." People that Jim's life has influenced are spread throughout the fifty states and around the globe, dispersed in schools, banks, hospitals, prisons, universities, fire stations, factories, orphanages, seminaries, police departments, resorts, businesses, hospices, virtually everywhere.

Over the years, by God's design, seedlings of Jim's work have fallen from the mother tree. Most of these seeds were scattered through the fifty states, but some were even blown abroad—out to every continent on this globe. Many of these seedlings sprouted;

225

some have taken root. Throughout our country and around the world there are young shoots, and offshoots of Jim's work, struggling up through the hard ground of non-acceptance and indifference. Most of these saplings go unwatered and unfed, unattended by human hands, just as the mother tree was when she too was a sapling.

As for offshore projects, in many countries and cultures there is little or no tradition of charitable giving, possibly due to the absence of tax deductions as incentive. Even in cultures known for their hospitality and warmth, there is little historical precedent to financially support not-for-profit projects. Works that will bless lives, nations, and the world sometimes struggle to survive. Usually, most of these "labors of love" are young and unknown, as Jim's work was not so very long ago.

The Jim Rayburn Foundation has been birthed to be a blessing, not only to the mother tree, but to saplings that spring forth from her as well—a foundation sowing not simply financial blessings, as God enables us, but in the words of St. Francis of Assisi:

Where there is hatred . . . let us sow love
Where there is injury . . . pardon
Where there is doubt . . . faith
Where there is despair . . . hope
Where there is darkness . . . light
Where there is sadness . . . joy

May we not so much seek to be consoled . . . as to console
To be understood as to understand
To be loved . . . as to love
for
It is in giving . . . that we receive;
It is in pardoning . . . that we are pardoned
It is in dying . . . that we are born to Eternal Life.

Join us. Let the dance begin.

Jim Rayburn (III)
jimrayburn@compuserve.com
www.jimrayburn.com

Give the Gift of
From Bondage To Liberty
to Your Friends and Colleagues

CHECK YOUR LEADING BOOKSTORE OR ORDER HERE

❏ **YES**, I want _____ copies of *From Bondage to Liberty* at $17.95 each, plus $3 shipping per book (Colorado residents please add $1.26 sales tax per book). Canadian orders must be accompanied by a postal money order in U.S. funds. Allow 15 days for delivery.

My check or money order for $_____ is enclosed.

Name _____

Organization _____

Address _____

City/State/Zip _____

Phone _____

Card #_____ Exp. Date _____

Signature _____

Please make your check payable and return to:
Morningstar Press
1947 Forest Ridge Drive
Colorado Springs, CO 80918